Out My Backyard

Canoeing West from Wisconsin

#001 Scene in the Missouri Breaks, Montana

by
James B. Kurz

If your book is missing the CD,
make a copy from another book
or send $3 and your address to:

Last Gasp Publishing Co.
James Kurz
N4015 Sisters Farm Road
Ladysmith, WI 54848
715-532-7246
www.sistersfarm.com

ISBN 978-0-9823873-0-6

Printed in the United States of America by
Publishers ExpressPress, Ladysmith, WI

First Printing: March 2009

Out My Backyard

Canoeing West from Wisconsin

by
James B. Kurz

Preface 1

My impossible goal is to write a book about my trip that will be as good as the trip itself. I am writing this preface in March, 2006, 11 months after setting off, 4 months after returning to Wisconsin. I can see the Flambeau River through my window; it has been open for weeks. The call is stronger now that I know where it can lead. Give it a rest, I tell myself–the flowages will be iced over for another month.

#619

Out My Backyard, Canoeing West from Wisconsin

Preface 2
March, 2008

I have concentrated on writing this book for the last 2 months. It has been a joy reliving the trip through the photos and my journal. I came to realize that to even approach my goal of writing a book as good as the trip, I needed to display pictures, lots of pictures.

The goals of the book are close to the goals of the trip (discounting comfort, survival, etc): To show the transition from leafless Wisconsin in April, through effusing Minnesota and South Dakota in spring, through the dry fields and erosion of the Dakotas and eastern Montana in summer, to the schizoid mountains of Montana in early fall, parts dry, parts wet. To show beauty and surprise wherever I found them. To simply document the nature of the land, of the people, and of me, beautiful or not.

Pictures do all of this so much better than words that I have included 779 of them on the enclosed CD. To keep costs and paper use down, 490 photos are shown in the book to give the reader a good grounding on the area discussed in the text; these photos are small and in black and white but are indexed the same as the color photos on the CD. I have also included the number and caption for the photos on the CD not displayed in the book, though, taking a cue from obnoxious sports commentators, sometimes there is no caption. I hope you take the time to inspect these photos in color as you read the book by inserting the CD in a DVD player or computer; both devices usually have slide show and pause capabilities. If your book is missing the CD, make a copy from another book or send $3 and your address to me at N4015 Sisters Farm Road, Ladysmith WI 54848.

I sincerely hope you enjoy this effort, a poor man's coffee table book covering an exciting canoe trip in a beautiful part of our world in 2005.

Jim Kurz

Table of Contents

Out My Backyard, Canoeing West from Wisconsin

Chapter 1

The Flambeau

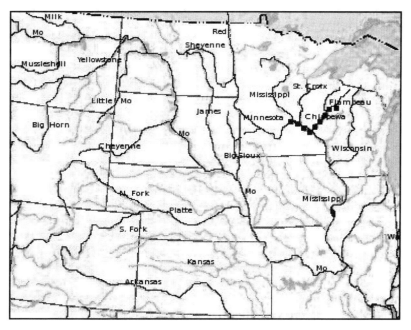

#002 Canoeing the Flambeau, Chippewa, and Mississippi Rivers

Yes, the essentials would fit if I emptied the dog food pail into a plastic bag and lay the bag on top of the other 5 gallon pails, 7 of them: the dried apples, the buffalo jerky, the dried mixed vegetables, the flours, the dried milk, cous-cous and macaroni with cheese pail, the oatmeal, oat bran, and whatever pail, and the tool with medicine kit pail. I cleaned the kitchen cupboards of canned goods, bottles of spaghetti sauce, Ramen noodles, and more whatever, hoping the box containing these things would stay dry until I ate things up. The large cooler filled up easily with the 4 quarts of pecans I had shelled, the 5 boxes of fish coating, 2 pots, 3 metal cups, venison sausage from Tom, cheese, bread, peanut butter and even more whatever. Clothes were in the backpack stuck upright amongst the pails. Tents, sleeping bag, thermarest, plastic ground cloths, shotgun parts, wind-up radio, pillow, sleeping longjohns, water filter, were in my orange waterproof bag (with small leaks on its bottom side) bought years ago for whitewater canoeing. The sail, wrapped around the mast and boom was stuck in longways along with my two ten-foot poles and extra paddle. Sourdough starter and hiking boots out of sight under the front seat. A life jacket and a thick mat under the dog and a second jacket under the orange bag. Set of wheels stuck in and tied off. Lee boards attached and tightened up high for now. Rudder pinned in and pulled up. Bag of tennis shoes, butt pack of survival gear, new camera, small binoculars, new GPS, new cell phone, waterproof bag of atlases and highway maps of Minnesota, South Dakota, North Dakota, Montana, and Wyoming; tackle box, casting rod, spinning rod, shotgun shells, 4 bags of oak chips–hey, its a 17 foot canoe, not to worry.

#003 My back yard with trial load in canoe

Time to clean up the house before John comes at 10 for an article for the Ladysmith News. Funny how life circles incompletely. Twenty years ago in 1985 when I moved up here from Chapel Hill, John and I were part of the same bowling team, an old northern Wisconsin tradition but new to me. (Though I knew the joke–How do you tell the groom at a Polish wedding? He's the one with the clean bowling shirt.) We even went down to Madison for the state tournament, not that we were any good, just more tradition. But 3 years later when I was fired from the college, did my friend interview me for my side of the story? No, it would have violated their "good news or no news" policy. Ah well, John wasn't editor then. Anyway, here's some policy-consistent news and here's John. We had a good interview and he took some pictures. By the time we were finished, Marita, Brad, Tony, Kevin, and George had arrived. They all guffawed at the amount of stuff and weight of some of the pails as they helped me carry all of it the 150 yards to the river. I repacked the canoe pretty much as before and stuck in 4 gallons of water and other things here and there with the dog food and now 2 boxes of canned goods on top, leaving the front end open for Daisy and just enough room for my feet. A few pictures, hearty good wishes, a consensual shaking of the heads and by 11:15 I was off!

#004 Heavily loaded, but on the water

#005 First view downriver on the Flambeau of Wisconsin

Two hundred yards down I tied up and walked back to the house for a final look around and to thank George for doing my vacuuming. I gave him the last 3 of my 800 pounds of New Mexico pecans and the perishable food Kevin had forgotten and returned to the canoe.

I well knew that this might be the best part of the trip, maybe the only downstream canoeing in a wonderful, now mosquito-free, part of the world. So I immediately got into vacation mode, ready to take what might come and enjoy it if possible. I played with my Pentax Optio 33WR digital camera, trying to figure it out without the manual son Nate hadn't included with the camera. I got a nice shot of Ruth's house, let Daisy run along the shore for a while, and, with the wind behind me, even sailed down the reservoir to the Thornapple dam, my third canoe sailing experience.

I had tested my new wheels on pavement with Daisy in the empty canoe and declared it a good system. Still, not wanting to stress the system, I left less than 100 pounds in the canoe as I wheeled it down the gravel to the water below the dam. I hadn't gone more than 30 feet when the canoe sagged to one side–I had hit some sand on the right side to stop that wheel while the other wheel kept going and twisted the frame between the wheels into trash.

#006 Bummer!

I had thought about this trip long enough to know that this wouldn't stop me–I had a yoke for carrying the canoe on my shoulders, a backpack, straps on the orange bag, handles on the pails. But still, if I was actually going interstate past Minnesota, there would be some 5 to 10 mile portages. Without wheels those portages could take a week with all the stuff I have. Well, I would probably have a lot less by the middle of the first long portage. I can think about that later, I confided to no one. It took 10 trips and 2.5 hours for the 100 yard portage but I was floating again by 4:30.

I couldn't quite see Bob's old cabin on County E because of the islands, but smiled to think of him and the good times catching northern pike and small muskies and roasting turkeys when we were teaching together back in the 80's. And smiled again to think of my lawyer's polite cynicism at our assurances that Bob would confirm my side of the evidence in my suit against the college for breach of contract, the lawyer's doubt because Bob was still employed at the Mount Senario. He did, of course, and so did Joe. Another, smaller, smile as I remembered my winnings--half for the lawyer and half for a used station wagon.

#007 Pretty birch trees on the Flambeau

Time to think about wheels. Erle Barber can fix anything metal but there is a welder also in Holcombe, closer than Ladysmith. I would have to do better than the original though, reinforce the aluminum, maybe add bearings. Silk purse out of a sow's ear comes to mind. Maybe make something sturdy from scratch and send it ahead of me. I was still in Rusk County so I had plenty of options, maybe too many. I'll bet Joe Flater will know the welder and maybe give me a ride there or back home.

6

I knew Joe a little, seeing him 3 or 4 times in 20 years. I had played basketball and volleyball with Austin, one of his 3 sons. He has sponsored the Flater Triathlon for years, run-bike-canoe, which I had so far unfortunately missed. I had watched a couple of Packer games with some friends at his tavern at the junction of the Flambeau and the Chippewa. One time his wife was tending bar and the conversation got into something about fences, swinging gates, misunderstandings, intentions, accusations and court suits. Somewhere in there Linda chuckled at the idea that Joe had even one mean bone in his body. This was just a little after my divorce and I easily picked up on and remembered that even Joe's wife thought he was a good guy.

I tied up the canoe and Daisy on the Flambeau side of the bar, and eventually found Joe inside. He had just returned from guiding a fully successful turkey hunt for 3 clients. But, between taking care of them and their trophies, he found time for another turkey in need of wheels. (Another joke, this one from Ivan Doig, who usually sets his books in Montana–"Do you still carry a dead turkey under your arm for spare parts?") I could sense what I found later to be the universal fisherman's response to my story, his ears perked, his eyes brightened, lips curled into a little smile as I told him my bold plan and showed him my pretty dog, full canoe with sail rig, and homemade paddle. We discussed my broken wheels and options for all of 2 minutes when he said "Here, take mine." He showed me his sturdy steel-framed set of 16 inch bicycle wheels that he sometimes used to push boats and motors up the hill at the end of a certain float trip he guides on the upper Flambeau, the whitewater section.

You could have knocked me over with a feather! I had researched wheels on the Internet and hadn't heard of anything close to these and here he was offering to lend them to me. It was getting dark, so he showed me where I could camp and we talked a little more inside, where he showed me a trophy muskie on the wall that he had caught within half a mile of where I live. He was proud of the catch of course but even prouder that the "fish" on the wall was just a replica and the real fish was still swimming in the river. I gave him a check for $100 for his (under) estimate of the cost of the wheels, thanked him to the point of his embarrassment, and paddled the canoe around to the Chippewa side to camp. I had a hard time fighting the current even for that 100 feet up to the camp site and finally resorted to one of my poles to push me past the fastest part. I set up my new tent in the dark, thankful that I had practiced the setup previously in daylight.

My rudder worked well for sailing, giving me a hand for steering and another hand for holding the sheet (sailor lingo for the rope attached to the boom), but with all the weight in the canoe (probably about 700 pounds), I couldn't raise the rudder entirely out of the water; this caused steering problems when I paddled. Deciding to take off the rudder, I dropped the only pin I had into the clean but dark river water. Well maybe Joe had a cure for that, too. Linda found me his strong underwater diving light and I found the pin after a few minutes. Returning the light, Linda, a few tavern persona and I discussed the chances of a successful trip and the merits of the main characters, given the broken wheel frame, the difficulty in going upstream, the lost pin, and the heavily loaded canoe. They all thought Daisy was doing her part real well.

Chapter 2

The Chippewa

Thursday, April 14. I slept fairly well with my old sleeping bag and my thermarest, staying warm even though there was frost in the morning. I was up and gone by 7, took a break at 8:30 at the County Highway D bridge on Lake Holcombe to dry the tent and eat something. I think that was the first time to use my wood stove.

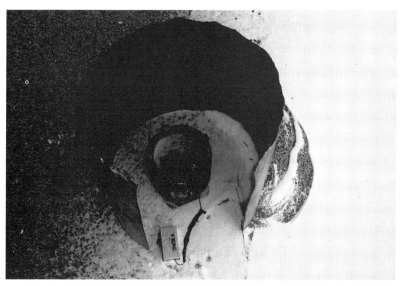

#008 Sierra Zip wood cooking stove

It is a 4 inch diameter double walled bowl with a fan underneath that blows air into the space between the walls which then feeds the fire inside. The fan runs off of a single AA battery encased in a little box that also contains a 3 position switch, low, off, and high. It seemed to work well frying the eggs that morning. A little burning stick fell on the ground near the stove and started the leaves on fire. I figured a controlled and observed burn would clear out the leaves so there would be no surprises later. True, but I had forgotten about the wires between the switch and the stove. First time to use my tool pail to find the electrician's tape to reinsulate the wires.

#009 Goose nest

The wind was against me all day. I had taken my canoe out twice to practice sailing as soon as the ice had gone out and had been able to sail into the wind somewhat with the near empty canoe. Couldn't do it today but didn't know if it was lack of wind or the heaviness of the canoe. By sailing to the right of the head wind and then to the left one can make one's way upwind, called tacking upwind. So I paddled against the light wind on Lake Holcombe, no current.

#010 Pretty lunch site

#011 First lunch plus thumb, new camera

I saw a bald eagle this day and a lot of waterfowl–mallards, common mergansers, wood ducks (recognized by their sound during takeoff), and Canada geese. I didn't have a Wisconsin atlas with me and the highway map was no help–I "explored" a dead end bay, found directions from a friendly resident, and paddled over to the dam. The wheels worked great under the canoe, even on the dirt or grass path of the portage. I found a nice camp site halfway through the quarter mile portage and brought the rest of my baggage there with 5 more trips. Played with my GPS around the dam and measured a 30 foot drop. I took a waypoint at my campsite as I did on my first night. The GPS unit indicated 7 miles between my campsites and 10 miles made the first day, from my house down to Flater's Resort. I could see that if I made a waypoint for each campsite, I could measure the straight line distance traveled each day and then get a minimum on total distance by adding up all these line segments. Since the river here travels in a fairly straight line, the river miles, straight line miles and highway miles are pretty close to each other. I was pretty tired that second night and slept well.

Friday, April 15. I was awoken by sand hill cranes by 7 and finished the portage easily but got my feet wet getting in the canoe. My left hand was starting to crack and stiffen. Also

#012 Portage system, Cornell dam

portaged the Cornell dam without problems though I couldn't get down to the water with wheels. I had to drag the canoe over the rock.

#013 Difficult rocks below dam

There were 2 noisy rapids below the Cornell dam. I ran them easily but hitting a rock could have been a disaster in that cold water, especially if the front had perhaps hung up and then the back had swung around and hit a second rock. I was able to tack upwind today for about 1 and 1/2 miles, changing directions about 10 times. It would have been faster just paddling but it was good practice. I was having problems with the leeboards. They keep the canoe from sliding downwind when tacking, but I can't keep them always tightened in the down position in case shallow water might break them, and they don't do much good loose as they practically float on the water. I can't reach them from inside the canoe because they are right behind the front seat. Daisy's job of course, but she doesn't seem to care. So for now I'll only put them down when I can get to them by standing on something like a dock and want to go up or cross wind in deep water. They are not needed going down or nearly down wind. The currents below the dams do not last long. I pulled into shore within sight of the old bridge near Jim Falls, on the left side. Made 12 miles camp to camp, straight line.

Saturday, April 16. I was up by 6:30 with a little rain, left by 7. It is a funny place–you canoe past a dam on your right which may be the overflow dam, while most of the water goes through the power house and dam at the end of the narrow but deep water on the left. I took out at the only grassy spot among rocks on the left, emptied the canoe and dragged it up the bank to a path along the top of the bank which led to a portage path across a wide grassy gentle slope about a half mile to the lower water.

#014 Snow below old Jim Falls area bridge

14

#015 Final portage path, Jim Falls dam

It took 6 trips again, and I picked up some wood along the way to help slide the canoe the last 30 feet of rock. Before starting out I took a walk around the town and had a skillet breakfast at the Junction Cafe for $5.50 plus tax, real nice and real hungry. The owner had no "no clue" as to the naming of Jim Falls. An older gentleman there could remember that they used to have a canoe race once a year from Ladysmith to Jim Falls or perhaps further down. I was on my way by 1 and hit my first rain by 2, soaked by 5. I couldn't get to my raincoat without stopping and figured I'd paddle hard enough to stay warm. I did for a while but I was pretty cold by the time I stopped under the County S bridge. I heated water for cocoa and had a nice lunch, watching a curious mink under the bridge. The rain stopped with still some daylight so, in my warm clothes, I paddled down to the portage sign to the right of the Wissota dam and camped right there, with just enough time to check out the portage before dark, i.e. sleep time. Made 10 miles.

#016 Rock outcropping on Lake Wissota

#017 Drying out; didn't work

Sunday, April 17. I continued to hang my wet clothes and added the tent to try to dry in the morning but the fog stayed around for hours. The portage was about 7/8 of a mile, long enough to make me think about efficiency. I noticed a discarded pallet and using my ballpeen hammer and Peace Corps vice grips grabbed up 3 thin boards, 4 inches by 4 feet and placed 2 of them on top of the frame of the wheels. Placing the cooler on top of these boards left about 9 inches sticking out on both ends, enough to support 2 pails. I strapped the cooler to the wheel frame and slid the third board under the straps on top of the cooler and through the handles of the pails using this board as a handle for my second trip down the portage. My handle didn't give me much leverage when the load would shift a little or on going up or down hill. I made one trip with the lightly loaded canoe and 2 more trips with packs and such for a total of 4 trips, down from 10 at the first portage and 6 at the previous 3 portages. I met Mary Schaffer and her husband, and Lee and Jean from the Chippewa Falls area using the hiking trails in the park around the portage.

It was just a couple of miles to the Chippewa Falls dam and an easy portage across Court Street about 200 yards to Duncan Creek which flows into the river below the dam. On the bridge over the creek a blond lady with a dog (Judy Ganzer) took time to ask me about my trip, and then intercepted me downriver with a reporter (Jeff Hage) with camera. The people I met from Chippewa Falls sent me the newspaper clipping from the Chippewa Falls paper. I meant to take out in Mount Simon Park in Eau Claire but missed the boat landing in the dark and ended up right at the dam and paper mill. I found a large concrete pillar with steps of sorts, and went to sleep on its top.

Monday, April 18. I repacked at 2 a.m. when it rained, slept again for an hour when it stopped, repacked again with the rain at about 4 and stayed up until daylight at 6. I scouted a route around and somewhat through the paper mill back to the river with help from some of the employees up to the point of asking who had the key for a gate to a fence downriver. When the manager, Steve Enders, husband of my best student during my 3 year stint at the college, heard I was there, he came around with a pickup truck and 5 other guys and took me down to the next boat landing, 2 carrys; Jana had told him I was on the way. One of the helpers was a good friend of Joe Flater. They turned the hardest portage into the easiest.

Drifting below Eau Claire turned to paddling as the wind, with foot and a half waves, came up. I took a rest on a cushion on the rocks for an hour while a noisy airboat went up and down the river. I paddled against the wind until 5 and pulled out to make my first chocolate tapioca pudding (see recipe appendix) with lots of pecans, excellent. The wind subsided and I drifted to a campsite on the right at about 8 p.m. I tried calling son Nate but lost contact. Today I had seen 7 eagles, 2 beavers, and a few ducks. Made 10 miles.

#018 Ella, on the Chippewa, south of Durand

Tuesday, April 19. I awoke at 6:50 to the raucous tunes of geese and turkeys. A flock of geese took off after I had finished my leftover pudding breakfast. It rained from 11 to 5 as I paddled and drifted to Durand and shopped for milk, brownies, honeynut cheerios, oranges, bananas, chips. I camped at Ella, where we used to cross over into Beef Slough, an offshoot of the river that meanders for 20 miles on its east side and dribbles into the Mississippi rather than rejoining the Chippewa.

After returning to Wisconsin in 1985 Bob Boettcher, Joe Ruthgeerts, Nate and I spent some fun times here deer hunting, shotgun and slugs. It is a wonderful part of the Tiffany State Wildlife Area. We have a picture of most of the 13 grandkids of my parents jumping off the abandoned railroad bridge into the deepest part of the slough. Good fishing for smallmouth bass, northern, catfish. I couldn't work it into my route this time. At Ella I found the source of most of the air boats in the area–the Anderson brothers. One of them was in their auto repair shop constructing the support structures which would go onto the 8 foot wide boats that come from Florida. I gave him $10 to help maintain the nice park and boat launch. I called a few people including brother Joe who said he was going to send a solar charger for my cell phone. I also called my home phone to see if I had any messages and to change my answering message giving a 30 second report on the trip; I had told people to call my home phone to find information that way. I charged the cell phone battery at the outside outlet of the Anderson shop and slept without a tent on top of the picnic table in the shelter. Made 21 miles.

Wednesday, April 20. As I was packing to leave, Chris from Minnesota put in his boat to go up to his cabin which has no road access. He was going to turkey hunt and fish for red horse. Fishing had been good lately as it usually is in the spring. He gave me a box of Malt-O-Meal cheerios from the company where his dad works; he would have given me more if I had had the space. I got off by 8 and noted that I had seen 3 eagles by 8:15, including one with a fish. With the wind behind me, good current, and Minnesota bluffs in the distance, I made the 8 miles to Highway 35 in 2 hours, paddling just a little relishing the last current in my direction for a long while.

#019 First interstate view, Minnesota in the distance

I knew of a slough that cut over almost to Lake Pepin and took it rather than following the Chippewa all the way down to the Mississippi at Wabasha, Minnesota. It was a picturesque river bottom area with the St. Paul to Chicago railroad tracks and bridge passing through.

#020 Slough to Lake Pepin

#021 The Burlington Northern & Santa Fe railroad

#023 Mississippi bottomland

As I approached Lake Pepin, I could sense the wind behind me, so I pulled over and stepped onto some tree roots to set the leeboards down and started sailing up the lake. I could see the water ripping past the canoe with the sail full out and wondered how fast I was sailing. Then I looked at the shore and realized I wasn't going anywhere! I was actually on the upper part of the river rather than the lower part of the lake–there was a lot of flooding but I had found the main Mississippi! By stepping on the boom sheet with my foot and leaning my back against the square handle of the rudder to steer, I managed to sail, steer and paddle the 100 yards necessary to surmount the worst current and then did sail up the lake.

Southwest Wisconsin is probably the prettiest part of the state, with the river, the backwaters, their bluffs, and the hilly terrain away from the river, alternating between hardwood forests and rich farmland. My Bohemian dad grew up in Durand, my Norwegian mom in Menomonie, North Menomonie where all the Norskies lived. After 20 years of marriage, mostly in Port Edwards in the center of the state, they built a cottage on a dredged canal connected to Lake Pepin. The cottage was sold after my dad died in 1994, but I stopped to see it anyway and talked to Pete Pavlosi who knew my dad and his big northern story. I had spent some fine summers here in my high school days.

#024 The old Kurz family cottage

#025 Klampe's Hill with geese in the air, Bogus Creek area

I sailed to Stockholm and spent the night in the park. I saw my first 50 pelicans there and met Theo Rick who was excited about going to some wilderness schools with Tom Brown, renown tracker. Made 18 GPS miles but this included a big curve south and then west.

#026 Submerged jetty near Stockholm Wisconsin

#027 Barges on Lake Pepin, same place

Chapter 3

The Mississippi

Thursday, April 21. The morning dawned cold enough to require an extra sweatshirt. The wind was with me again but stirring up some good-sized waves. I had canoed in the Boundary Waters of Minnesota across some big windy lakes and had a lot of faith in 17 foot canoes, but didn't know quite what to expect with a big sail and a big load. The system worked well this day with a reasonable wind and reasonable waves, even when I decided I had to cross the lake near Maiden Rock; I knew I didn't want to continue sailing to the end of the lake and then paddle or sail crosswise to those waves in shallow water.

#028 Maiden Rock or another bluff just like it

#029 High water on Lake Pepin

I then paddled and sailed about 2 miles up the river and rested above a point on the left and as the wind died down I paddled until 5, mentally and physically exhausted from dealing with waves, wind, and sail and from just sitting up straight for 8 hours. Made 12 miles.

Friday, April 22. I called last night's camp the "Angry Beaver Campsite". I counted 27 splashes around 9:30 p.m. At one point the beaver was only 15 feet off shore and may have splashed water on Daisy; at least she growled after one close splash. I was up at 6:45 and off by 7:30 with no wind but a lot of current. Big wind came up soon, right against me. I tried to use it by tacking but of course this eventually led me out into the fastest current. I lost ground (well, position) whenever I changed directions as I tacked back and forth and sometimes the wind would die and leave me powerless mid-current; I was better off paddling along the shore. Moral: winds can be useful, but the current is relentless. I pulled out about 3:30, pretty tired. Made 5 miles.

Saturday, April 22. I awoke to frost and 27 degrees according to my windup radio, 10 to 25 mph N to NW winds. It was already windy from the predicted direction, my direction. Stopped in at Evert's Resort near Trenton, in view of the dam and lock #3, ready for a new experience. Steve Vick, the manager, treated me to a pop and Snickers and called up the Army Corps of Engineers at the dam. Tim Fuller told him I could "lock up" with my canoe, but he was worried about the other end. It turns out that 10 days ago, the day I started (April 13), a tug with 8 barges (3x3 abreast with one missing back right) sent the barges through the lock, came through with the tug boat, and retied to the barges. (The lock has a winch that can pull the tugless barges through and above the lock; there isn't room for a length of 3 plus the tugboat or for any more than 3 across. Thus the maximum size is 15 barges, a set of 9 going through first and then the tug and the back 6.) The lock is located on a curve of the river and the water is moving towards the dam and flood gates on the right as one emerges from the lock going upstream. The Mississippi had been in flood then and still was now; Steve figured the water level now was about 6 feet higher than winter level. Tim said the volume was 46,000 cubic feet per second now with normal winter flow of 8,000 and summer flow of 10-15,000 cfs. Some boaters were taking their motorboats right through the flood gates, a drop of about a foot. No wonder I was making slow progress! When the barges of April 13 emerged from the locks into the current, the tug couldn't keep the front barges from going right, possibly because of the missing barge in back. Cables broke from the stress of trying and 2 barges went through the gates, the others wedging against the gates. Tim was thankful it hadn't been a lot worse. He said the problem with the current starts at about 20,000 cfs.

He took me around on an electric cart to show me the current and the possible portage through flooded woods and soft dirt and grass. I could picture myself bottoming out in the woods, carrying parcels by hand through the shallow water and mud; the loaded canoe was way too heavy to drag over almost any resistance. I appreciated his concern of course, but I figured I could do what the tug couldn't–I could turn around and come back into the protected lock area, since there were about 200 yards of current before the flood gates. Tim locked me up and I'm sure was watching me as I paddled through the protected area where the barges would be tied up waiting for the tugboat to come through. The current was minimal on the shore edge as I left protection and I had no trouble continuing along the shore.

The problem started on the other side of a docking area about a half mile up. It is easy for a brisk wind to stir up big waves when the wind blows against the current; I've seen it many times. But this wind was churning up big waves blowing downstream.

#030 Windbound, looking downstream towards the lock on the right

#031 Looking upstream at the nuclear plant

I rested there about an hour observing waves, current, and wind while I ate up the last of Tom Lee's venison sausage gift. The fudge from Delaine was long gone. The end of my left arm was more like a curlable club than a hand. I considered going home and planting my garden... Naah, this was way too much fun.

I figured that if I could get past the dock, I could paddle up a slough on the left and camp there even if it was a dead end. With some hard paddling I made the slough around noon and yes, it was a dead end but a good camp. I was on Prairie Island and took a couple hikes upriver towards the nuclear power plant to stay warm and keep my legs functional and to the main channel occasionally in the afternoon and took some more pictures. Towards evening a tugboat came up through the locks and escorted a set of barges and tugboat into the lock, pushing on the front end barges to keep them away from the flood gates. Made 4 miles.

#033 Tug boats under a full moon

Sunday, April 24. I got going by 7:30 with a brisk but manageable wind against me which picked up through the day. I crossed without much trouble but a lot of effort and came up the north side, along the railroad tracks until the inside of the curve looked better.

#034 Barges and bluffs

Continuing slowly along the south shore (the river is coming from the west more than the north in this area), I came to a natural protrusion that would have forced me into the main current and I could tell I wouldn't make it. The other side looked more reasonable so I headed across. I realized later that the whole river narrowed at that protrusion to maybe half width and the current coming through was horrendous, giving me a roller coaster ride in 5 foot rolling waves–I was "Rolling, rolling on the river!" Luckily the waves were more than a canoe length apart and as long as I went with the current, I remained stable. However the reason for being there at all was to cross and I crept sideways as quickly as I could before being swept too far downstream. I probably lost about 100 yards which I viewed as a generous compromise. When I canoed back up to the constricted area again, I could see that it was no better than the other side except that this side was flooded, and by chopping though a 10 inch log with my hatchet I was able to wade the canoe past the problem area. I found one more spot like that; rather than investigate the other side, I portaged the heavier stuff about 100 yards and camped mid-portage with a supper of cous-cous, my dried veggies and pudding. Made 8 miles.

Monday, April 25. Had leftover pudding for breakfast. Without the heavier stuff, I was barely able to canoe past the big logs that were part of the problem, after a failed try where the mast hit an overhanging branch.

#035 Part of an intrusion from the north side

#036 My portaging path, on logs, same site

After canoeing up and reloading I got going by 9 and was at a Prescott marina by 11. It was kind of a private docking area but I knew I wasn't harming anything by using it. I was relieved to see that the gate opened to let me out but then alarmed to realize that it was constructed to keep dummies like me out, not in. I figured I could climb over the gate if necessary but I met a nice marina guy on the way out and it was opened for me by the time I had eaten brats, Hershey bar, Mountain Dew and popcorn in Prescott WI. On my way up to Hastings MN I saw an eagle catch and then drop a 15 inch fish. Terry and Jim let me tie up at the Hastings Marina. Nice people and nice place–their outside bathroom was always open and had a shower. I called Bob, my college roommate for 2 years, about 1:30 and he picked me up around 4:30 after his workday at 3M. I spent a wonderful, warm evening and night at his house in Stillwater about 20 miles north of Hastings. Dean, our hunting buddy with land north of Cumberland Wisconsin, came over for a visit before I showered, shaved and konked out for the night. 5 miles

#038 Bob Boettcher (right) and Dean Hansen

Tuesday, April 26. After an easy breakfast with Bob and Margaret, Bob dropped me off at the marina by 8 and I went through lock #2 soon thereafter, a rise of about 5 feet this time. Windy day with choppy water below and above the lock. I turned towards the left shore as soon as I cleared the lock and grounded immediately 50 yards from the shoreline with my end of the canoe in deep water parallel to a brisk wind driving foot and a half waves. I had no alternative but to back stroke quickly before I got turned sideways to those waves but I knew what was likely going to happen 5 seconds before it did–a good size wave came right over the back of the canoe and drenched me back to toe. Well, OK, I didn't get drenched, it was just one wave. It could have been refreshing if it hadn't been 40 degrees in the air and colder in the water. It rained on me 8 times that day. I camped on the north side of the current and saw an immense sand dredging system on several walks that evening as I tried to warm up. This helped to explain the many barges filled with sand I had been seeing. Made 8 miles.

#039 Pretty, rocky ravine on west side

#040 Sentinels on a sand hill

#041 Sand pumping system

#042 Sand-laden barges

Wednesday, April 27. At 7:30 a.m., my radio reported 34 degrees with snow flurries, strong wind against me again. Paddled from 9:30 to 6:30 but treated myself to lunch at the Inver Grove Heights Marina. Towards evening I ran into a huge logjam that pushed me way out into the current; the other side looked inhospitable as it was lined with barges.

#043 Log jam

#044 St. Paul at a distance

#045 St. Paul, close up

I could have portaged, but I barely managed to paddle around it, using the logs to help me rest occasionally. Camped again on the north side on shifting land near Pig's Eye Lake. I had read a little history of early Minnesota and knew at least that Pig's Eye was the name of a trader with a post in this area around Fort Snelling; apparently at least one eye was not real attractive. Made 9 miles.

Thursday, April 28. I was paddling by 8:30 a.m., entering the St. Paul downtown river area around noon.

The current was surmountable with merely hard paddling along the shore, but single barges tied up along the edge would push me out further into harder paddling and double barges were a real challenge without a rest possible along their smooth sides, though a couple of times I rested between barges if they were double length as well as double width. I found the Minnesota River around 2:30 and went a few hundred yards past it to the Watergate Marina by 3. I had made a few phone calls and managed to meet up with Bucki family, friends of our family; Richard and Cindy who have a cabin in Ladysmith but otherwise live in St. Paul; and Julie, a daughter in the family of the original sail owner, with her sister's partner Jay.

#046 Cindy, Richard, and the Bucki family

Julie gave me a wonderful care package in a sturdy little canvas bag with velcro closure which I used the rest of the trip to store my straps used to secure the canoe on my wheels; the original contents were cherished and eaten the next day. She was delighted to see the sail rig put to use again.

#047 Julie and Jay

Jon Bucki had bicycled with my son Nate about 5000 miles in the summer, fall, winter and spring of 1994 and 1995. They also left from Ladysmith, passed through New Ulm, Minnesota as I would and then struck out for the west, passing through South Dakota, Nebraska, Colorado, Utah, Arizona, New Mexico, Texas, Mardi Gras in New Orleans, Alabama, Georgia, South Carolina, stayed with Mike Su in North Carolina, and eventually to Western Massachusetts, where Nate registered for the next year's fall term at Williams College. Our 2 families had met up with the boys in Arizona before they took a leave of absence from their bikes and traveled through Mexico, Guatemala and Belize by bus, train, and thumb. 10 years later Jon was walking with a cane due to a spinal fistula but said he was improving. Jennifer was her usual charming self and the 2 boys stomped in the mud puddles around the marina. The marina manager Andy acted like this happened all the time, let me tie up overnight without charge, and fed me popcorn while I waited for my friends.

Richard and Cindy showed me a view of Fort Snelling, took me out to eat at a Chinese restaurant, let me catch up on email somewhat, and put me on their couch for the night. Made 6 miles.

#048 Fort Snelling from across the Mississippi, St. Paul, Minnesota

#049 Fort Snelling, close up

Friday, April 29. Cindy dropped me off at the marina by about 8 where I canoed upriver a little to a slough that cut over to the Minnesota, along which there was a park and the lower entrance to Fort Snelling. I was about to pay for a tour of the fort when I realized I was without wallet, cash and credit cards included. I got Cindy on the phone and she went home after her first cleaning job, found my wallet next to the computer, and brought it over to me at the fort. I had started a tour of the fort with some school kids from Minnesota but found I couldn't enjoy it, not knowing where my wallet was, and evidently preferred pacing back and forth in front of the fort. Back on the river, I passed under the Mendota Bridge carrying Minnesota Highway 55, built in 1926 and, keeping only the arches, rebuilt in 1994. Soon after that I took some pictures and movie of the jets coming right over me on their way to land at the Minneapolis airport. Made 10 miles from noon to 7.

#050 The Mendota Bridge, St. Paul

#051 Close to the Twin Cities Airport

Chapter 4

The Minnesota

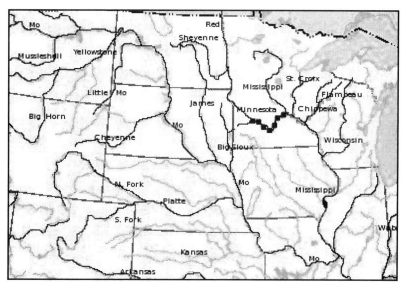

#052 Canoeing the Minnesota River

Saturday, April 30 showed me muddy banks nearly everywhere; I had to find a downed tree in the water for docking unless I wanted an ankle-deep mud bath.

Barges were frequent, but only as far as Port Cargill, in the town of Savage, Minnesota. Lest you think the town was named as a description of its inhabitants, it was named after a Mr. Savage in 1904 who owned a famous race horse, Dan Patch. I assumed, as I canoed by, that Port Cargill was named for and owned by the

#053 Mud, a lot

#054 Lunch stop on the Minnesota

big grain exporter, Cargill and all it meant to me was that I wouldn't have to deal with any more barges. Well, that is all true but the least interesting historically. The Cargill Company made 18 ships for the Navy in World War II at Port Cargill! They were ocean going tankers of type A.O.G. and were used as auxiliary supply ships. The first one slid sideways into the Minnesota River in 1942, righted itself squarely in the water to everyone's relief, and was commissioned as the USS Agawam at New Orleans on December 18, 1943.

#055 USS Agawam, passing under the Mendota Bridge, 1942

It hauled fuel and supplies with a crew of 125 and 16 big guns in the Solomon Islands during the war, and around Yokohama and Shanghai afterwards. It was overhauled in San Pedro California and then saw service in Guam, Hawaii, Alaska, the Philipines, and Viet Nam, decommissioned in 1957.

If you compare this last picture with #050, five pictures back, you might wonder, as I did, how that warship had enough water to float under the bridge. My picture in 2005 showed very little water; in fact I was on an almost currentless shortcut from the Mississippi past the southern reaches of Fort Snelling over to the Minnesota, above its main current. It was all too new and confusing to me at the time. Turns out that the Minnesota cut a new channel one year, and is now east of the bridge, a rather frustrating turn of events for engineers, I assume.

These days Port Cargill is just one of 30 river ports owned by Cargill and the only river port in Minnesota and Wisconsin not directly on the Mississippi River, those others being Minneapolis, St. Paul, Red Wing, Winona, and La Crosse. The future of barges on the Mississippi is a little cloudy right now, but for simply moving large and heavy stuff they can't be beaten. It is 5 times as fuel efficient as trucking. One barge can hold as much as 15 railroad cars or 60 semi-trucks. As fuel gets more expensive and green house gas reduction attains the importance it deserves, river traffic might increase. Of course it is slow, and seasonal around here. It requires government maintenance of the 9 foot channel (which may have to be deepened), of the locks (which may have to be lengthened) and of the dams. The barges, the maintenance, and the structures themselves often conflict with other river uses and threaten river wildlife. One pessimistic report points out that as Brazil develops their agriculture, their lower prices due to lower labor costs, cheaper land, and a deeper river that requires no locks will undercut the U.S. export market so badly that there won't be a demand for better or even continued mass grain transport in the Midwest.

I saw 3 beavers today and met a fisherman with a 13 inch drum, alias freshwater sheepshead. (Totally unrelated to the ocean sheepshead, e.g. this one has no teeth; the shape of the foreheads suggests a sheep according to one Internet source.) The river level seemed to be dropping but current was like yesterday or faster. I found a nice sandbank a few miles above Shakopee and pulled over to camp. Made 10 miles in 8 hours.

#056 Daisy

#057 I prefer sand over mud, probably always

Sunday, May 1. I had made contact with brother Jon's wife's sister in Carver and Rene' offered to bring me a meal at the bridge where son Cody and friends would be fishing. A quick look at the map found Carver a few miles away and I took off for lunch at about 8:45. Current was unforgiving and by the railroad bridge, logs had channeled the current such that I barely made it through; a portage would have been hard carrying through the flooded woods. It snowed on me 3 times and rained once, the weather it was fine.

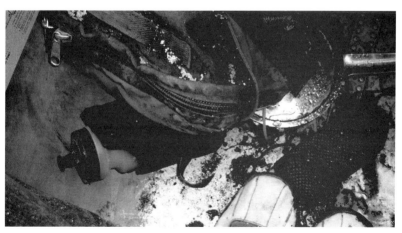

#058 A little snow

Bob had given me some plastic gloves in which I kept my left hand constantly in order to moisturize it. After a few days the inside of the glove had a dead flesh smell but I was able to actually grab the paddle rather than use the hollow between thumb and fingers as a pivot. My left hand has had a circulation problem, especially to the index finger, ever since I cut into it at the base of the fingers on a table saw when I was 9.

Hungry, tired already of paddling, and cold, I took a better look at the map and saw that the only highway bridge ahead was still about 5 miles away, straight line miles at that. It turned out that they lived close to this bridge on the far side of Carver. I called Cody a couple of times to try to let him know I would be late. It came to me how much I enjoyed my lack of schedule on previous days, i.e. eat when hungry, rest when tired. I was probably the most tired of the whole trip when I sighted the bridge and kids at 5:45. Cody was gone but he had started digging an anti-boredom hole which was now over 5 feet deep.

#059 You probably couldn't pay them to do it!

His friends caught one little sturgeon while I was there. Rene' and her mother Jeanie brought a wonderful, now cold, lunch down to the bridge, took a good look at me, pushed me into their car and brought me home for a warm shower and then warm supper. Not that I was too cold or needed a little love and care of course, I wwwould have bbbeeen just ffffine. Cody drove me back to the bridge where his friends were watching Daisy and he and I talked by the campfire until 11. I set up my tent under the bridge and slept well. Made 10 miles in 9 hours.

#060 Rene' and the family Essig

Monday, May 2, I got a cold start by 8:45. Stopped after a half mile to walk back to get Daisy's dish, nice walk. Midmorning we walked 3/4 mile into Belle Plain to get a few supplies. Stopped a half mile down from there to walk back to get the 12-pack of Mountain Dew I left lying in the rocks by the bridge. Lousy walk through mud at the bridge end, both ways.

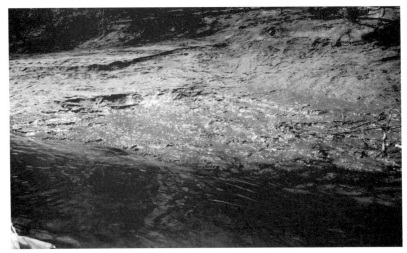

#061 Example of mud

#062 You compare, mud versus sand

I stopped midday at a lovely rock projection for a sunsoak and to make pudding. My journal notes were washed out somewhat here from using washable ink and journal dunking. Saw whole family of 4 large beavers under the tree roots, practicing their synchronized diving performance. Made 8 miles.

Tuesday morning, May 3, there was frost on the tent. Had a nice break with the last of Rene's casserole and Bob's sausage on a wonderfully firm sand bank. Mozzarella cheese, store bread, and water for a late lunch, 2 peanut rolls and 2 Dews for snacks. Climbed a hill at camp with views of spring flowers, the river, and a neat Minnesota farm near the top on the far side of the hill. Made 7 miles.

#063 Occasional impenetrable willow thickets

#064 Trout lily a.k.a. dogtooth violet

#065 Minnesota River through the trees, on CD only

#066 Minnesota farmer's paradise

Wednesday, May 4. I started out by 8:30 a.m. My journal noted that the river and I are both wearing out. River seemed a little lower, less flooding. I walked into Henderson and got 2 gallons of water and camped a couple of miles downstream from Le Sueur. Made 6 miles in 10 hours.

#067 Walking tree

#068 Another mudless lunch stop

Thursday, May 5 was my first day without long underwear! All day! The high was probably in the 70's. I docked at the boat launch in the park and walked into Le Sueur about 11 am. I bought a new pin-on compass, tube repair kit for my wheels, and candy bars at the hardware store. While they let me charge my cell phone at the hardware store, I ate 2 brats and a Dr. Pepper at SuperAmerica, and took a tour with Ann Little of the Le Sueur Museum. Topics included a refurbished dental or doctor's office and the history of Green Giant Foods; I took a picture of the Giant outside the museum. I caught up a little on my email at the library and Jan helped me find the name of the guy in Mankato (Brand Frentz) who helped Verlen Kruger write his book about his 28,000 mile canoe trip across and recross North America (The Ultimate Canoe Challenge). I gave him a call that night with my recharged phone and arranged to meet him.

#069 The symbol of Green Giant Foods

Jan also suggested I stop in at the newspaper office which I did on my way back to the river. I had a pleasant interview with Malcolm Maxwell, a farmer turned reporter at age 56, 8 years ago. He liked the name of my canoe, Clueless on a Lark, a play on the names Lewis and Clark and a mild chiding of all 3 of us. Malcolm kept wanting to know why I was on a trip, noting my "calloused, cracked grime-laden hands. The former college professor, house painter, and molecular biologist is canoeing from Ladysmith, Wisconsin to Montana..." I gave him three tepid reasons, adventure, curiosity, and the chance to promote human-powered recreation, but admitted I was still working on an answer.

#070 Clueless on a Lark, fully loaded

Le Sueur, St. Peter, and New Ulm were all on my path and were all involved in the Indian War of 1862. Fort Snelling was actually created in 1819 to keep settlers off of Indian lands which included all of Minnesota. But while Minnesota was a territory between 1849 and 1858, the Dakota tribe of the Sioux Indians (Sisseton and Wahpeton bands) were forced into signing a treaty in 1852 giving up rights to everything but a reservation to the west and north of New Ulm. When Minnesota became a state in 1858, the reservation was reduced further to just the west side of the river. The treaty included promises of supplies every year. The government reneged often on the supplies for over 9 years; the only reason it worked at all was that the money for supplies came through the traders who would allow (often unfair) credit, knowing they would be paid eventually. When the tribes convinced the Indian Agency to give them the money directly, the traders stopped giving credit. When the money didn't arrive and the Indians were starving, one of the traders even said "Let them eat grass." The hungry Indians began killing and robbing even fellow church members while allowing whites they liked to remain alive. The store owner quoted above was found dead with grass in his mouth.

Between 450 and 800 white settlers and soldiers and an unknown number of Indians were killed in the 6 week war. 303 Dakota Sioux were convicted of murder and rape in quick trials, but President Lincoln pardoned most of them as war combatants; 38 were hung in Mankato on December 26, 1862. The rest of the Dakota were expelled to Nebraska and South Dakota, and the Minnesota reservations were abolished. A few Dakota were allowed back into Minnesota later. This uprising of 1862 could be considered as the beginning of Indian wars that continued more to the west until 1890, with the biggest victory for the Indians in 1876 at Custer's Last Stand.

Getting back to 2005, I remembered to retrieve my cell phone and put in a few hours paddling upriver beyond LeSueur, named for an early French explorer. Made 6 miles.

Friday, May 6 was enlivened by our first "dog overboard". Towards midday Daisy tired of watching the near shore and lay down for a nap facing the other way. She just got a glimpse of a huge beaver jumping in with a big splash, jumped up to turn around, and slipped on the aluminum seat right into the water. I already knew that dogs have just a little sense of shame but no capacity for guilt; embarrassment does not seem to be felt either. She just swam to shore, shook, and hopped back in when I gave her the chance. Nice warm day, looking for shade. About mid-afternoon a boat came up from behind me on their way to Mankato, stopped to talk, and offered me a beer. I thanked them but said "I'm from Wisconsin, I only drink milk," and then explained how I dislike beer even though it seems to be the favorite beverage of everybody else in Wisconsin. They got a chuckle out of that and headed upstream. The mud was extreme here, with 4 to 8 feet high steep banks with no shore, no rocks, no sand. Towards late evening I was finally forced to pick a bank that had a little shore next to a 3 foot bank and set up camp. I was about to look for wet wood to cook I don't know what, when the guys in the power boat came back down the river and gave me a big bratwurst and a quart of milk! What a treat. Noticed the first mosquitoes, but I was safe in my tent. Made 10 miles in 10 hours.

#072 The whole forest on the move

Saturday, May 7, it rained about 7 a.m. so I slept in, all packed up by 10. As I was loading the canoe the little shelf slipped into the river and I was up to my knees in mud and cold water; bad start. It rained from 11 to 12 with a brisk wind in my face until I turned the corner in Mankato, the place you can instantly see on the map: going upstream you change from southwest to

#073 Even mud can amaze

northwest. Later at home I ordered the book *Le Sueur, Town on the River* from the museum and found that the reason for this 90 degree turn is the presence of bedrock that refuses to erode. If you continue upstream you will come to the South Dakota border and then start heading north until the Minnesota (which used to be known as the St. Peter) peters out and, with some portaging depending on water levels, you would reach Lake Traverse. If you canoe to the north end of Lake Traverse, there is an outlet that would take you downstream to the Red River and thence to Lake Winnipeg and Hudson Bay. They call this the Red River of the North, I think to distinguish it from the river with the same name in Texas, though there is a third one on the western Kentucky/Tennessee border, and another in Wisconsin. In some years and in the spring, steamboats would try to make it from the Minnesota to the Red, but the one year they perhaps could have, no one tried it. But I wasn't going that far, just another 50 miles or so to Redwood Falls and then west up the Redwood River.

I had 10 minutes of sailing after I turned the Mankato corner until the wind pooped out. As I was approaching the entrance of the Blue Earth River coming from the south and Iowa, I stopped to talk to a young fisherman who said they might need some help up ahead near a power boat. I didn't see any cause for alarm from that distance but I hustled up there a little faster than my usual end of day speed. I am glad I did. What I found was a 4 year old boy in the power boat which was anchored in the fast water coming out of the Blue Earth and downstream was a young father without a life jacket up to his neck in deep water holding onto his 2 year old girl in her life jacket with his right hand and onto a dead snag (i.e. a mostly sunken dead tree) with his left hand, everybody safe for the moment, but wondering what to do next. He couldn't swim back upstream to the boat with her and of course couldn't leave her there and swim by himself. I guess he could have swum towards the point between the rivers with her, the one armed crawl, but the current might have swept them past the point and out into the Minnesota where he would have to make it to shore from 50 yards out. And if he did make it to shore he would still have kids in 2 places. I hovered next to him for 20 seconds explaining that I didn't have room for both of them but we quickly agreed to put the 2 year old between my legs and then while he was holding the canoe there we agreed that I would paddle and he would swim back to the boat while still holding on to the canoe. We didn't make much headway together; seemed like we were each a drag on the other. He felt he could swim back to the boat by himself; I was worried that his adrenalin rush would die out and he would sink like a stone after leaving the canoe and told him that if he got tired he should float back to me. But he got back to and into the boat easily and I brought him his daughter. He was very thankful and I was happy I could help. The wetness started when, with no warning, teenygirl got it in her head to jump out the back.

My friend Dick Dannenberg from graduate shool days was waiting for me at Land of Memories Park a half mile further up. He and Sally usually come down to Mankato from New Ulm each Saturday for dinner out. They had done that already and brought me a tub of KFC. Oh my goodness. We talked while I ate and then took a walk past the boat launch where the wife had joined the 2 swimmers and son; they thanked me again. Dick and Sally said "see ya later" and left for home. I put up my tent. I was tired. Made 8 miles in 9 hours, 13 river miles.

Sunday, May 8, Mother's Day, reminded me that I didn't have one any more; Annette Shirley Brekke Kurz died of Alzheimer's Disease in 2003. She was no longer herself within 3 years of my dad's death in 1994. This was the lady who had her own Indian motorcycle when she was 17. She would have approved of my trip and hopefully this book, as she was a writer also.

There is a plaque here in Land of Memories Park that commemorates the hangings mentioned above and adds the hope that Indian-White relationships can evolve to something better.

I had chicken for breakfast, lunch and supper, and Daisy crunched all the bones. Well aware of my high cholesterol levels as a possible problem, I even ate most of the skin, believing that I would burn off any fat I ingested.

#074 Killdeer on the mud, on CD only

About 11 a.m. I pulled out to a sand bar (sand and gravel was becoming common now) to chat with Brand Frentz and Joe Michael who had canoed down to see me.

#075 Joe Michael and Brand Frentz (right)

They are both members of the local Mankato Paddling and Outing Club and what they now told me about the upper Missouri encouraged me even more to go have a looksee. We took some pictures and chatted about my trip and of the one Brand helped write about. I don't think it will surprise him to read here that Kruger's trip was mostly valuable to me as a rotten way to experience a river, trying to keep to schedules with long hours, no hikes, and setting arbitrary records. We did discuss how Kruger and Landick had an immense problem getting from the Headwaters of the Mississippi over to the Red River because of the low water, log jams, and beaver dams. I had taken heed of that miserable time for them, knowing that I was traveling heavier. Thus the only scouting I did was in the far southwestern Minnesota area, hoping my memory of past road trips in that area was correct that, while there might not be much water near the divide, there weren't many trees either. That appeared to be true in the area I scouted.

Brand and Joe paddled with me back up to their different putins. Brand and I traded paddles for a while and we both laughed–My old home-made white ash paddle (1.9 lb) was probably 3 times the weight of his new angled plastic paddle, and my newer paddle (2.5 lbs) even heavier. We laughed again when he pointed out that I was using his new paddle backwards. (For the record, I did have it right side up.) When we got to Michael Creek, skinny old Brand picked up his plastic canoe onto his shoulders and walked right up the hill towards his house. When he isn't canoeing or writing he is a personal injury lawyer, fairly well known it seems. The Club invited me to Mankato after the trip to give a slide show, a very nice time with new friends.

The wind was fickle but with me after we parted ways, so I sailed as much as possible because I was still tired from yesterday.

#076 Another tree leaving the bank, on CD only

Later on I could hear thunder and as the wind died to nothing, I quickly made camp on a well used fishing point next

#077 Very large erratic, an apt name for large
rocks before people knew about glaciers

to a creek about a mile up from Judson. I had the tent up just in time for a quick hard thunderstorm. About 8 fisherpeople and mushroom pickers came by later in the evening and early morning, catching pre-season northern, walleye, and, further upstream the next day, small sturgeon and catfish, all of which were returned unharmed. Made 8 miles.

#078 Sturgeon

#079 Underside of sturgeon, a bottom feeder, on CD only

Monday, May 9. I was on the river from 8 to 5:30 with about 2 or 3 miles of sailing. Two brothers, Michael and Tim, river rats from Mankato, shared Hawaiian Punch and orange juice with me and were going to give Daisy some bacon pieces but I got most of that too. Rained on me 5 times. I camped at Courtland Park near where Dick used to live. The cooler fell off my shoulder as I was setting up camp, dumping all my hitherto dry contents into the muddy water. Worst victim was a quart of shelled pecans which eventually molded entirely. I walked into Courtland and bought some candy bars. Made 7 miles.

Tuesday, May 10 was a typical day fighting the current and probably the wind, but my notes got washed out. I had a surprise visit from Joe Michael, Ron Burly, and Dale who were canoeing down from New Ulm. Joe was paddling an expensive but fast canoe engineered by Kruger. I had good energy the whole day, but got a further boost when, above the Cottonwood River which came in from the south, the Minnesota slowed down to what seemed to me as close to nothing. Now, the same amount of water has to pass by every inch of river between tributaries, but if the bed widens and deepens, the surface current can be pretty slow. If there was a wind in the morning, it had died to nothing, not a ripple. My body had hardened to a paddling machine with all this upriver, upwind nonsense. I just let it rip for an hour, watching the shoreline whip by! (At, what, 4 miles per hour?) I passed under a scenic river view with an old railroad bridge.

#080 Railroad bridge below New Ulm

I canoed all the way to the west end of New Ulm and gave Dick a call. He picked me up at about 5 p.m. We emptied the canoe and leaned it up against a tree at the landing. Dick's son Mike came down later with a padlock and chained it to the tree. Dick and Sally fed me, we all looked at the pictures on my camera through Mike's computer and my USB cable, and Mike, the computer wizard and truck and car builder at age 17, made me a CD of the pictures. The kid sparked like a Tesla coil; he was enrolled at South Dakota State in Brookings for engineering in the fall. Let it be known that I have nothing bad to say about warm houses and soft beds. Made 7 miles.

Wednesday, May 11. I shaved for the second time on the trip. Dick had the day off from his opthalmology practice in preparation for a turkey hunt in Wyoming. We drove around New Ulm in the rain and wind and cold, checking in at the Department of Natural Resources (DNR) for maps of the Minnesota River and found a very nice series of 4 maps covering the whole river. I talked to Bob Kahl there about my trip; the secretaries were more interested than he was. I bought a 12 volt recharging plugin and cable to recharge my cell phone off of the solar panel brother Joe had sent to Dick. We copied my journal at Dick's office and sent the copies and the CD to Polly. We left a message for river keeper environmentalist Scott Sparlin to see if my trip could somehow help create interest in cleaning up the rivers in the area, especially the muddy Cottonwood, but never heard back. Back home I dried and repacked all my clothes, made pudding for the family, and had a nice talk with Dick and Mike.

After getting a Ph. D. in Molecular Biology at Vanderbilt a year after I did, Dick went on to their medical school and eventually into the eye business like his older brother; not bad for a couple of blue collar Germans from Milwaukee. He and I used to waterfowl and rabbit hunt together in Tennessee; we hardly ever got anything, canoeing for ducks and geese, but we always had a good time. We remembered how one trip when it was his turn to go back and get the car, I let him and the bicycle off and I canoed on to meet him further downstream. I swear I didn't know I left him on an island! He shouldered the bike and waded across up to his waist I think. Another time we left predawn, drove 2 hours, waited for geese that never came close, drove back for a noon seminar, and fell asleep in the warm, dark back of the lecture room. 0 miles

Thursday, May 12. The rain was coming down as 10 inches of snow in the Black Hills. The outfitter claimed only an inch of snow on the other side in Wyoming, so Dick left for his hunt. The outfitter was right and Dick got a turkey the next day. Mike took me along to Glencoe to pick up a part for his "mudder" truck and we had a nice talk while the wind raged and the rain fell sideways.

We took a little tour of the town. New Ulm was settled mostly by Germans and in honor of German stubbornness, they put up a statue in 1897 similar to the one in Detmold, Germany honoring Arminius of the Cherusci.

#081 Hermann the German, in New Ulm

Arminius led a coalition of German tribes that wiped out 3 Roman Legions in A.D. 9, so he was one of the barbarians that helped curb the Roman empire though it lasted another 500 years. Apparently the coalition didn't include the Vandals; in fact, in a bit of sad irony, some modern day vandals turned on old Hermann and put bullet holes in his statue.

Mike dropped me off at the river at about 1 p.m. and I made use of the wind for an hour and a half when it died. I was accompanied by pelicans as usual. Temperature was 39 degrees at start, about 42 for a high, rain, and then thunderstorm at 6 p.m. Ugly. Made 6 miles in 5 hours.

#082 Pelicans

Friday, May 13, one month out. I canoed from 9 to 7 against a strong head wind all day. The current was back to fast due to 4 days of rain. I noticed Eight Mile Creek was very muddy. One of my new maps indicated a canoe launch at Harkins store. Always looking for an excuse to get out of the canoe, I looked over the site. After a few years of river business before the railroad through New Ulm and 31 years of serving the farming community, the store was closed down in the 1901, with a full inventory of goods for sale. The descendants have kept it that way and now it is a state historic site and museum, open on Sundays with local history presentations; but it was closed today. The river had evidently made the canoe launch site a joke—about an 8 foot drop straight down; I had to canoe 150 yards further upstream to find a place to beach the canoe.

Further above there was a maze of islands but, with the river in flood, I didn't enter any dead ends. I never saw the Hinderman Bridge either. My new maps weren't much help. Made 8 miles.

Saturday, May 14, I stayed in the tent until noon as the wind raged and the rain fell. I canoed from 12:30 to 6:30 against the wind but without rain except for sprinkles. I invented my own wind scale, thinking back to the beginning of memorable wind. In increasing order it is Negligible, Angry, Pissed Off, Really Pissed Off, i.e. the NAPORPO scale. Today it was RPO. I took a pudding break under the Highway 4 bridge and got checked by 2 Minnesota game wardens. It was the first day of the season for walleyes; I guess it speaks well for Minnesota people that I was the best suspect for law breaking they could come up with. (My favorite quote about the state: "Minnesotans take moderation to an extreme.") Understandably doubly disappointed in not arresting anybody yet that morning and not finding any fish near me (my gear was at the bottom of the canoe, still unused), they hadn't much interest in my trip.

The river was again divided upstream from the bridge. I went left successfully the first time, the second time found a dead end, the third time a log jam. I suspect my learned advice to take the first left and the next two rights will be useless next year as the river floods have their way with the land. The sand and gravel had disappeared and the river was back to all mud. I camped on Fort Ridgley State Park as soon as I saw the signs. Daisy jumped a pheasant during our evening walk. Made 4 miles.

Sunday, May 15. I was canoeing by 8:15 against a weak wind. The Minnesota was starting to look pretty nice. Took pictures of a fisherman with a carp and a drum and of a lovely lunch spot.

#083 Mossy rock, on CD only

#084 Standard deer hunting cap

#085 Pretty lunch spot

#086 Pretty river

I happened by just as Lisa Pfeffer caught a 26 .5 inch walleye. She returned the fish to the river, so I told her I'd send her a picture to remember the catch (and did).

#087 Nice fish!

#088 Pretty area, with rocks, on CD only

I was still a little tired paddling but stronger than the last couple of days. Felt even better after a long walk into Franklin where I spent $20 on chicken, cherry Pepsi, eggs, milk, bread, candy bars. I easily justified the candy as I had told Ruth and Ralph in Ladysmith that I would spend their $10 gift on chocolate. Saw 3 bold rock outcroppings in what was otherwise a shore of mud, along with deer, eagles, geese, ducks, especially wood ducks. Made 8 miles in 10 hours but with a one hour nap.

Monday, May 16, I canoed from 9 to 7:30. The wind was generally with me from the southeast, but fickle. I was able to sail about 3 miles. At one point the river was so fast and narrow that I think I would have had to have gotten out and waded the boat up; but I sailed right through with no problem. Then I turned the corner and lost the wind and had to paddle hard to keep from going back into the fast water. Saw first 6 goslings, about egg size, and mosquitoes again. Took a short walk into Morton and spent $5. A fisherman from Franklin recommended portaging before the railroad bridge on the Redwood River because there was a fast curvy section just above there. I camped below a rocky projection that was actually causing a whirlpool, nice spot. Made 9 miles.

#089 Camp view

Tuesday, May 17. It rained until 10, so I started about 11 and got to the junction with the Redwood about 1 p.m. Arrived at highway and RR bridge about 1:30 and decided to see what the river was like; figured I could always drift back down and then portage. I hadn't figured on the deceit of the river–the first half mile wasn't bad, high water with one small rapids through some curves and high walls and then flat. And then one rapids I had to wade through, no big deal, better than going back down and portaging. Then another, and another, for a total of about 15 rapids stumbling over a rocky bottom in water up to my waist. Five hours later I made it to the first park in Redwood Falls.

#090 Redwood River rapids downstream of Redwood Falls

#091 View in park, Alexander Ramsey Park

I had met Jim Doering through my Internet investigation of the Redwood River, and he came down to see me along with Eric Posz from the Redwood Gazette. Eric wrote a nice article with a big picture on their front page of me looking over my rudder as I prepared for camp. The picture shows me wet almost to my armpits. He was a little loose on the details, having me coming up the Cottonwood to get to the Redwood and implying 7 pails of food rather than 3.

Jim and his daughter Ashland took me home to meet his wife Shelly and daughter Kylie where I got washed, warmed and fed nicely. We charged my phone and washed some clothes and dried nearly all of them. Jim gave me a nice water proof bag which I used to advantage the rest of the trip, especially for my hiking boots and extra tennis shoes. Made 2 miles in 7.5 hours.

Chapter 5

The Redwood

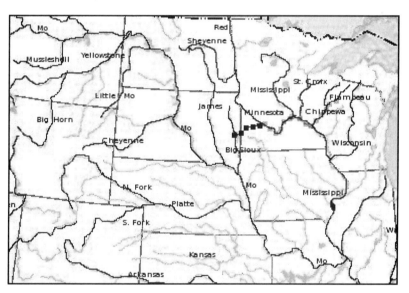

#092 Canoeing the Redwood River and Flandreau Creek

Wednesday, May 18, 2005. Rained again overnight. I took out the heavier cargo and brought the canoe to the tent site while drying out. Paid $20 for 2 nights of camping here in Redwood Falls. Met Lever Deprez walking his dog Mollie in the park. He came over from Belgium in 1952 at the age of 23. He farmed outside of town and raised a family; his wife died a few years ago, and he now lives alone a few blocks from the dam and lake on the other side of the hill. He agreed to let me cache some stuff at his house, so I got his address. I took the cooler and 2 pails on wheels and carried 1 pail up the 3/4 mile of steep hill and down a little to his house. The dam, bridge and falls are all close together between his neighborhood and the rest of the town of Redwood Falls.

#093 Lever, Mollie, Daisy

#094 The Falls these days

I hiked across the bridge to town and visited Glen Madsen at his Veterinary office; he had gone to Vet school with the vet from Ladysmith, Julian Lang. I was going to buy some dog food until I found that he sold special dog food at a special price; he and his staff then gave me 2 boxes (all I could carry) of free samples wonderfully packed in waterproof packets. I had a lunch at Burger King with dessert at Dairy Queen, living high on the hog.

I stopped in to see Jim Doering at his office for the Redwood and Cottonwood Clean River Coalition and I encouraged him to continue the cleanup of these river systems. He gave me a RCCRC cap, a sweatshirt, and a ride back to camp. It threatened more rain all day and finally sprinkled a little at about 7 pm as I pulled the canoe over the hump to Lever's house. I hooked the canoe front to the back of my back pack but the canoe fought back by jerking me up and down, besides having to take off the backpack just to rest, since I couldn't reach the snap. While I always tried to place the wheels in the middle of the canoe and pack symmetrically, one end was always a little heavier. I came to simply pick up the heavier end with either hand and walk alongside while pulling the canoe uphill or on the level; on the downhills, I would turn it around so I'd be pulling back. This turned out to be the steepest pull on the whole trip, resting about 10 times. At first the rests were incomplete, keeping the canoe from rolling away, but I soon learned to come to rest where I could butt the downhill end of the canoe against something or tie up the uphill end. I had packed the first load inside Lever's garage but I left the canoe outside overnight–Hey, this is Minnesota. I saw a pretty falls on a side stream just a little off the trail on the way back during the sprinkle. Lever gave me flat, dry, tasty Belgian cookies made by his daughter which I had with milk for supper.

Thursday, May 19. Up by 7:45, made my oatmeal while drying the tent bottom, backpacked over the hump to the lake landing, made a couple of short trips from Lever's house, and was on Lake Redwood by 11. Lever and Kelly from Jim's office came to see me off. This was the first night and next day without rain in 10 days, warming to about 75 degrees. Canoeing the first flat water since Lake Pepin was a short 3 mile treat., then rapids and wet feet about every half mile, no problem with delightfully calm and scenic interludes. Used my recharged cell phone for a second interview with Megan Parker of the Eau Claire, Wisconsin based Country Today newspaper. She wrote a nice article about my trip which I saw later. Saw first pheasant chicks, discovered by Daisy. Made 7 miles in 7 hours.

#095 Portage party

#096 Typical rapids above Redwood Falls

#097 Nice river

#098 Not really as small as it looks here

Friday, May 20, I was on the water from 9 to 7. The river was gaining some personality with interactive shorelines and pastoral sections.

#099 Welcome to western Minnesota!

#100 A glacial turd (erratic) in good current, on CD only

Nice day on the water. Camped next to a red cedar plantation and found a hunting camp with a collection of old cars, metal signs and license plates including a farmer's section, a picture of Babe Ruth and stiff competition from Popeye for his brand of soda.

#101 The Riverside Museum of Advertising History

#102 Close up

#103 We-no-nah canoes, Indian motorcycles,
Popeye selling pop, on CD only

#104 Babe Ruth says "Drink Red Rock Cola", on CD only

The lady owner happened by on her 4 wheeler and was sweet about letting me camp on her land, even though I pitched my tent on one of her roads. Lost kids trying to visit a friend in Vesta drove down that road around 11 pm. My attempt at giving them directions to Vesta was pretty silly since I knew almost nothing about roads in the area. Made 6 miles.

#105 Protect YOUR tree from rodents and deer!

Saturday, May 21. Big storm until 8:45 this morning. Dried out until 11. Talked to son of landowners and 3 friends as they canoed with beer from Vesta downriver on an overnight. After an easy paddle, I took a picture of fishing families at the Highway 10 bridge, then hiked about a half mile into Vesta. Had a pleasant chat with Jeremy at the Vesta Liquor Store, while he made me a double pepperoni 12 inch pizza for $8. What a treat! I also bought a 12 pack of Mountain Dew and some candy bars. Jeremy gave me matches, a roll of paper towels and some plastic bags. The Paskowitz kids and 2 cousins entertained Daisy while I was in the store and then gave me 2 gallons of water and 4 mint chocolate chip cookies as they helped me back to the bridge. I sent them 6 copies of the bridge picture in care of the local school principal. It turned out that they didn't attend the public school but rather a Christian school. They belong to a sect called the Plymouth Brother Christians. The principal got them the pictures anyway and they called to thank me later; I had a nice conversation with Russ, Leanne, and their father Randy.

#106 Vikings catching catfish

#107 New friends

I had a pleasant time on the Redwood above Redwood Falls. The water was a little on the murky side, which was discouraging because the smaller feeder streams were wonderfully clear.

#108 Clear side stream even after much rain

The current was medium to sometimes slow in the long pools with the occasional rapids that I could walk up, pulling the canoe. I sometimes stood up and poled with one of my two 10 foot white ash poles. Poling gave a better view and butt-relief and, with a 1 to 4 foot water depth, was probably a little faster than paddling or poddling, i.e. pushing off the bottom or shore with a paddle. But I found a day of poling hard on my arms and shoulders and had cramps in my right leg one night. So I just poled occasionally as a nice change from sitting down. This day, Saturday, I made 5 miles by GPS, 9 river miles according to a map Jim Doering had given me. The Redwood is curvy to the point just below exasperation.

Sunday, May 22. 25-30 mph wind from the northwest, confirmed by the radio, so I just poked along. The wildlife was especially entertaining here. Yesterday I saw lots of goslings that disappeared under water. Some came up next to the canoe and panicked, some came up next to shore and hid or sneaked along the overhang, and some never did come up! The adults would usually make a long, noisy exit trying to lead me away and, from their point of view, it seemed to work. But a few pairs would lay still near the far shore with their necks outstretched just over the water, trying to hide. This was a reasonable tactic if they were in grass or fallen logs, but "silly goose" otherwise.

I saw a medium sized raccoon swimming across the river and scared up 4 deer that were bedded down near the river edge. I looked 3 times near those beds, but never found any fawns. Beavers were plentiful, including a family of 3 sleeping under a root-laden overhang. The big mother dove under the canoe. Daisy had been trying to catch a beaver this whole trip and couldn't resist nabbing one of the little ones left behind. I'm sure the little guy was terrified but unhurt as I quickly retrieved him. As long as he was at hand and in hand, I took some pictures.

Also saw wood ducks and pheasant. I could tell the river flow was decreasing as it finally quit raining. A fisherman said it was

#109 Goslings near shore

#110 L'il beaver

down 5 inches from last weekend. The Redwood was small enough now that I found a downed tree reached all the way across. Daisy got into a fight later that night. Made 6 miles in 11 hours with an hour nap.

Monday, May 23. I took a long rest under a great blue heron rookery just west of Highway 6, trying to get a heron in the picture along with the 30 nests, failing. I saw lots of big carp today. Three Mile Creek, coming in from the north was really muddy, but the Redwood was pretty clear after that. I tried charging my cell phone with the solar panel brother Joe had sent to Dick in New Ulm, but the phone quickly indicated full charge even though it wasn't. I came to a beaver dam and camped mid-portage on a Minnesota Wildlife Management Area. 5 miles in 10 hours.

#112 Barely got under it

#113 Heron rookery

#114 4 foot beaver dam

Tuesday, May 24. I had to portage over a concrete bridge with culverts.

Seventy year old Gary used to deliver bread into South Dakota from Marshall. River really meanders here. Even though I was always looking to gather any mushrooms I might recognize, I hadn't found any yet. As I climbed up the river bank to find a camp site, I literally stumbled into a snack of asparagus which I ate raw; couldn't find any more. I camped just north of Marshall, near Highway 33. Made only 4 miles in 10 hours.

#115 Gary Deutz

Wednesday, May 25. Rained from 2 am to 5 pm, off and on. The river was higher already and muddy when I started, but then clear in Marshall, leading me to think that perhaps the storm sewer system was dumping in below Marshall. I poled from 11 to 1 into north Marshall. I scouted a quarter mile portage route to get around 2 small dams starting near the first ball park but before portaging first bought some food and visited the library in town. I found a copy of the Redwood Gazette with me on the front page, courtesy of Eric Posz. The portage took only an hour and a half with 2 carries. There were about 3 other places where I had to lighten the load before dragging the canoe through. I was able to pole through most of the Marshall meander, and even offered a ride for a quarter to a surprised lady in her backyard; she could tell it was just a flirtatious offer as there was no room in my gondola. I slept under a "No Camping" sign in the empty Lyon County fairgrounds on the west edge of Marshall, a nice spot with water and electricity on the back of some building to charge my cell phone. Made 3 miles in about 6 hours.

Thursday, May 26 was a nice day as I half poled, half walked the diminishing river. Good area for poling, saw the 10 pound carp better standing up, no other fish except minnows, but a number of snapping turtles.

#116 Gerber saws are sharp

#117 Variable river width

I saw a spot of yellow up ahead in a broad patch of weeds. My eyes seem perfect to me until I demand some detail; I couldn't understand what it was until at about 5 feet, I recognized the yellow underside of the neck of the biggest snapper in the world! I would guess the diameter of the neck was about 4 inches; I could not get a picture of this one before it quietly sunk away. My dad told me once of wading the lower Chippewa River sloughs in Wisconsin and stepping onto a rock for a better view. He was surprised when the rock moved him into deeper water.

#118 They get bigger!

I had to cut small trees twice to get through and trim branches in about 3 other spots. I had to almost empty the canoe to get over an 18 inch beaver dam. My meager pre-trip planning told me that the Redwood was canoeable through here, and with this much water it is, but no one had done it lately.

#119 Small beaver dam

The water was still up from yesterday's rain, but here, above Marshall, it was fairly clear, visibility of about 30 inches. I could see 5 inch suckers and maybe some small trout; the area ahead was supposed to be a trout stream. I was moving for over 11 hours from 8:30 am to 7:30 pm, seeing lots of deer. I took 2 lunch breaks, one of coprinus mushrooms fried with 6 eggs, my second scavenging. The last mile was mostly rocky rapids. Got hit with one short rain mixed with hail. Camped towards the upstream end of a half mile of new development with a few houses already. 4 miles

#120 Rocky but floats the canoe without me in it, on CD only

Friday, May 27. Got to the Highway 5 bridge in about 2 hours and had a nice walk into Lynd, with a bread and cheese picnic. Encountered significant rocks and current soon after in Camden State Park.

#122 Rocky and too shallow to float the canoe even without me

Walked and dragged for the afternoon until I arrived at the lower campground where I put $15 in an envelope and set up camp in # 24. Showered and shaved twice to get my money's worth. Scouted out the upstream trail in the evening. I met a family from near Watertown SD who had their own car repair business–Sherwin, Shelly, Ali, Caleb, and Gracie. They treated me to somores at their campfire that night, toasted graham crackers with Hershey bars and marshmallows. 3 miles

Saturday, May 28. Starting about 10 a.m., the whole family accompanied me to the horse camp at the south end of the park.

#123 Sherwin and family

I wheeled the cooler with 2 pails and wore the orange backpack; I had found that carrying even a light third pail soon became torture on my arms, even with switching sides. We went back to camp together also and they invited me for hot dogs and other fancy stuff like potato chips and catsup which I devoured.

I hoped to simply walk the lightened canoe up to the horse camp, but the river had too much drop and unforgiving rocks. I even altered the river course (i.e. moved some rocks) to get a better channel but ended up repeatedly almost emptying the canoe to get up umpteen drops. I wanted to enjoy the pretty trout stream but I wasn't appreciating it at all. I should have wheeled everything from the bridge between Lynd and the park all the way to Russell.

Of course Daisy had to walk as I struggled with the canoe. This hadn't been a problem before (other than chasing deer for too long), but now in the park, there were other people and dogs about and she left me twice that day. I found her walking with hikers the first time, noting that she surely heard me calling but refused to come until I was in her face. The second time I walked all the way to the highway entrance where the ranger drove me to the group camp where he knew they had an extra black dog. I tied her up that night at the horse camp and took her collar (with my name and address on it) off the next morning—If she didn't want to stay with me, I wasn't going to ruin my trip looking for her or being told in Montana that someone had found her in South Dakota. It is hard to know exactly what a dog understands, but she never left me again, on this trip anyway.

With the time wasted looking for Daisy, the morning portage, and the slow canoe drag, I only made 1.4 miles by GPS

Sunday, May 29. By the bridge on the south end of the park, I had convinced myself that the river changed character from rock to dirt and sand, and should thus be easier canoeing, but from there to Russell (2.4 miles by GPS) I counted 9 places that I had to lighten the canoe.

#124 Mid drag

The village allows free camping at the ball field on the west side above the second bridge. I walked upstream from camp to find the entrance of Coon Creek. Sitting on my couch back in Wisconsin with my Minnesota Atlas, I saw how Coon Creek could lead me to Dead Coon Lake in about 8 miles and to Lake Benton in another 7 miles, straight line miles not river miles. On the way back to camp, I got water from the Amoco convenience store, where the husband of the clerk offered to show me what Coon Creek looked like. We rode in his truck 2 or 3 miles up the creek, showing me that while Coon Creek wasn't rocky like the recent Redwood, it was smaller and shallow with riffles, occasional down trees, fences and culverts. And Highway 2 led straight to Lake Benton in only 12 miles, a no-brainer.

87

#125 Junction with Coon Creek

Monday, May 30. My trial portage around the falls in Redwood Falls had gone well with 3 trips and the one in Marshall well with just 2 trips. I worried that I'd jeopardize the rest of the trip if I broke my wheels or bent the canoe, so I decided to always make 2 trips per portage. So this morning I left my sleeping equipment at Russell and towed the canoe to Lake Benton with an extra 2 miles to get to Tyler City Park.

#126 Rolling

Lyon County 2 becomes Lincoln County 13, then I followed 111 south a mile and west a mile to the park on the lake. I left the loaded canoe there near some friendly campers and carried my wheels back with me straight east this time, a mile south of Highways 13 and 2, 170th Street I think. My feet were really tender from walking in the Redwood for 2 weeks and there was no good way to carry those wheels. I was flopped in the ditch in the only shade within a mile when along came a laughing Dave Norgaard with his Sturgis T-shirt. I perked up as he walked a mile with me, telling me about his pig farm, wind turbines he had helped the county build, and his biodiesel use. He invited me to hunt pheasants some time. I was tired and sore back in Russell. I had done my first marathon, 28 miles over and back in 13 hours in my hiking boots.

Several people stopped to talk to me during that morning, most of whom offered me a ride. One lady thought it so newsworthy that she called the editor of the Lake Benton News at home on this Memorial Day. Mark found me easily and we had a nice interview with pictures. 0 miles by GPS

Tuesday, May 31. I managed to improve my portaging technique, but I am embarrassed at the slow, step-at-a-time progress. I found that a short handle on the cooler on wheels was hard to balance as the slope would change how much pressure up or down I needed to apply and then slope plus a bump would shift the load. By tying my two 10 foot poles to the top of the cooler, I found I could pull and especially balance my second carry of cooler, 2 pails and the orange backpack easily, just like a rickshaw. I thus left both poles back in Russell when I pulled the canoe to Lake Benton. (This sounds pretty clever; but if I had brought one pole with me in the canoe, I could have pulled the empty wheels back instead of carrying them and still would have ended up with 2 poles in camp!)

#127 Pheasant eggs

#128 The corn is just sprouting

Anyhow, the third 14 mile trip took 7 hours and was much easier on my feet in tennis shoes. I saw lots of red winged blackbirds, including some yellow headed blackbirds, new to me. A young fellow was fishing off the pier at Lake Benton but catching just 4 inch bullheads and a 7 inch walleye. A campsite cost just $6 with water and electricity as I remember. Rain by 8 pm and calm after that. 12 miles GPS

Wednesday, June 1. I was planning on camping in the town of Lake Benton, so took my time getting going around noon. I had a nice crosswind mostly from the north and sailed most of the way southwest to the town. Had to stop and replace a broken bolt on the rudder with tools and an extra bolt from my tool pail. I saw the windmills on Buffalo Ridge.

#129 Ready to go

#130 Windpower, the current of the future, on CD only

Only took about 2 hours for 4.8 miles. Got a free paper with my article in it from the News office. Shopped for minute rice, oranges, banana, milk, candy, 20 pounds of dog food, and washed my clothes. Camped at the downtown picnic area with special permission from Steve, the town cop. Watched people catch more small bullheads, another 6 inch walleye, and one 9 inch crappie.

Going from one major drainage (The Minnesota) to another (The Big Sioux), one should expect an elevation between the two systems. Every such separation is unique, however, and this one involved the "Coteau des Prairies", literally "slope or hill of the prairie." My best description of this situation is that this uneven plateau separates the Minnesota not from the Big Sioux but from the James River, the next big river system to the west. It was evidently a big and flat plateau millions of years ago, but water not only flowed off its sides east and west but also the rain and melted snow that accumulated over the center of the plateau flowed south, creating a web of tributaries that now drain into a central river, the Big Sioux. (Yes, there is a Little Sioux also, which flows south out of western Iowa into the Missouri about 45 miles south of the Big Sioux junction with the Missouri which is at Sioux City.) The Coteau occupies parts of eastern South Dakota, southwestern Minnesota, and northwestern Iowa. The eastern edge of this Coteau seems to rise up fairly abruptly and is called Buffalo Ridge near the 3 state corner. Except for Camden State Park, the upriver approach of the Redwood River to Buffalo Ridge is a pretty constant slope, taking 65 miles to rise from Redwood Falls at 1044 feet to Lake Benton at 1746 feet, a gain of 4.5 feet per mile. (For comparison, the Missouri, Mississippi, and Minnesota rivers gain elevation at the rate of about a foot per mile.) But from the western edge of the lake to the top of Buffalo Ridge, there is a difference in elevation of another 150 feet in a distance of about a mile. Highway 75, however, led me south through a natural gap in the Ridge only 20 feet higher than the lake. The area on both sides of the Coteau were glaciated often, split by the Coteau into 2 lobes, "deepening the lowlands flanking the plateau" according to Wikipedia. I would guess the gap in the Ridge at Lake Benton was caused by some sort of glacier melt; certainly there is not now enough drainage to explain a 130 foot cut in the ridge, even if the lake were high enough to drain in that direction.

Thursday, June 2. I got up at 5:30 and left the town of Lake Benton by 7:30 with my canoe on wheels, leaving a 2nd load at the park. OK, I admit I was a little excited and I got up with the daylight—This was the day I would literally get over the hump,

#131 The time on my picture is 5:46 a.m.

92

away from the Mississippi! I had spent a few hours here last March, the only place I had scouted. I knew about the easy route on Highway 75 that led to a tributary of Flandreau Creek. If the water wasn't high enough there (hard to guess at in the snow of early March), I figured I would keep wheeling down gravel roads until I found enough water. This day I judged the water too low in this East Branch of Flandreau Creek as it crossed Highway 75, so I started west just before the crossing, about 6.5 miles from the park on County Road 89 in Pipestone County. I crossed the main branch of Flandreau Creek in about 1.7 miles and then turned south a quarter mile later onto 60th Avenue/County Road 76 and left the canoe under the bridge another quarter mile south where the 2 branches had already joined.

I took a brief lunch break and then, on the way back to Lake Benton, scouted an alternative route, north through Verdi and then east back to Highway 75 on Highway 9; the names of the rural highways seemed to be in the midst of change however. No stores in Verdi, one park. I towed my wheels back to the town of Lake Benton with one of my poles. I loaded up the cooler and

#132 Jim and Daisy at the Lake Benton News building

pails with the orange rubber packsack on top, stopped at the News office to ask them to take my picture, and hiked back through Verdi, my second marathon in 4 days, 26 miles and about 13 hours. I arrived at the bridge right at dark, exhausted but smiling. 8 miles by GPS.

#133 View downstream from bridge on Flandreau Creek

According to my GPS, I was 271 miles from home in a straight line (410 miles if you add up all the miles between campsites). This had taken me 50 days for an average of about 5 straight line miles a day. Using my thumb as a ruler on my USA map, I had gone 5 thumbs and needed to go another 10 to see the Montana border. Another 100 days would take June, July, and August. Don't rule it out yet!

Chapter 6

Flandreau Creek

Friday, June 3. It started raining soon after midnight and was still going strong at 9 a.m. No chance of a hot breakfast (i.e. oatmeal or pancakes) as there were no trees to supply wood for a fire, just grasses and crops. No buffalo chips either; and with all the rain the cowpies would burn about as well as if collected fresh from the cow. I packed up when the rain lessened a little and started pulling downstream. I was soon able to stand and pole, stepping out every one to two hundred yards to drag across rocks or gravel.

#134 Curvy, narrow, but floatable

#135 Pretty, shallows ahead, on CD only

I talked to 4 farmers, including Greg Buttman who saw me at a bridge. He said he had canoed it once to the town of Flandreau, but in higher water. When he said "It's my land for the next 3 miles, right into South Dakota," I was apprehensive about what he might say next, but he was just getting around to suggest where I might want to camp, which I did. It was close to a long unused railroad grade and missing bridge.

Daisy had been crossing the creek all day but when I crossed the last time in deeper water, she refused to swim across. When I hiked a half mile to the only tree to get firewood, I was sure she would cross to join me. When I put out her food, I was sure that she would cross to eat it. She spent the night on the other side. 6 miles

#136 Camp with nice view, last camp in Minnesota

#137 The firewood monopoly

Saturday, June 4. Rained overnight. Packed during a lull. In the morning mist the old bridge abutments stood out like Stonehenge in an English fog. There was a 5 foot dam to portage on the far side of the grade. Then a fun day of poling, stepping out about every 200 yards to drag, but pleasant sights.

#138 Minnesota Stonehenge

#140 Curious cows

#141 Curious horses

#142 The Guardian, on CD only

I wonder if flandreau is French for meander. Yesterday there were several places where I could see the path of the creek in the meadow, perhaps 50 yards out and 50 yards back, passing 20 feet to the southwest of itself. I didn't mind much–I had the Redwood River through Camden State Park still in vivid memory–This was a relatively easy gain of 20 feet, floated, not dragged. The current had an almost negligible effect, but still it was in my direction. No doubt the volume increased, but the creek bed probably also widened so that both days gave similar boating experiences–pleasant and moist, though it rained only intermittently on the afternoon of this day.

I had assumed there would have been some historic portage routes between the Minnesota and the Big Sioux, but I never found any mention of such a route in my library and Internet searches. The closest I came was a reference to Flandreau Creek as coming out of Lake Benton, an obvious error with Buffalo Ridge in the way. I forget now with whom I was discussing this when we realized the likely reason—Pioneers don't pioneer in canoes with long portages and fur traders don't make routes they don't need. Any trapper or trader on the Minnesota side could trade down the Minnesota and anyone on the South Dakota could trade down the Missouri.

I thus felt like a trail blazer, Daniel Boonkurz; I have serious doubts about having any followers however–maybe an historical buff/nut in 2105! The Mankato Canoe Club thought it was a first also; Brand Frentz wrote a flattering article on this portage for their magazine in 2006 (See Appendix 3).

I finally encountered some trees near the Big Sioux, including one I had to portage around over a sandy island and another I had to cut through. My whole body grinned as I aimed the canoe downstream on the Big Sioux. This river was certainly deep enough to avoid hitting bottom and the current was mild but with me! This hadn't happened since I started up the Mississippi 44 days ago.

#143 Junction with the Big Sioux

#144 Northern pike, first night on the Big Sioux

I hallooed somebody at the Country Club on the outskirts of Flandreau, inviting him to see me at the park he told me about. I parallel parked the canoe at the park next to a concrete landing. As the canoe rocked to a standstill, a 20 inch northern pike found himself cornered and jumped onto the landing. I had no fishing license yet, but more importantly I was tired, cold, and wet with good prospects of remaining so, even without cleaning, skinning and cooking a fish with wet wood; so back he went. It was still overcast with a medium wind but the rain had stopped. I decided to sleep under a pavilion roof in the picnic area and hung my tent and clothes out to dry. It turned out too humid to dry anything and then a light rain started at about 2 a.m. The continuing wind misted the pavilion wherever I moved my thermarest and sleeping bag; I would guess on a hot day that would have been refreshing.

I made a list at about this time of the animals I had seen over the last week or so—long-tailed weasel, mud and snapping turtles, deer, beaver, muskrat, opossum, raccoon, frogs, carp, northern. And birds—orioles, robin, little and great blue herons, starling, white egret, bittern, cormorant, large grebe, pheasant, mallard, wood duck, dove, kingfisher, goldfinch, king bird, geese, grackle, regular, red-winged and yellow-headed blackbirds, crow, various hawks I can't name, owls, vultures, Hungarian partridge, 2 kinds of swallows. Surprisingly no eagle since the Wisconsin/Minnesota border. 7 miles

Chapter 7

The Big Sioux

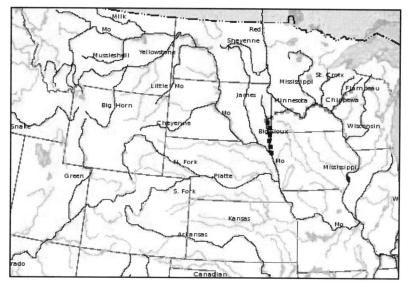

#145 Canoeing the Big Sioux River

Sunday, June 5. Jim Jepsen, who had been the friendly guy at the Country Club, and his wife Sue visited me at the park in the morning before or after their church time. They were friends of the Kirkegaards with whom I had corresponded before the trip regarding the canoeability of the river and their campground further downstream near Trenton. I was attempting to dry things out again without much success; Jim and Sue agreed it had been a moist month so far.

#146 Dam near the town of Flandreau

I left at 10:45 a.m. and immediately portaged a 7 foot dam in South Flandreau, a 45 minute task. Had a great float, including 3 exciting one-drop rapids. Arrived at the Double Bend campground at 5:45. Deb and Morris had gone fishing but left a note for me. Their daughter opened the camp store and sold me milk, graham crackers, Dr. Pepper, and bread. I was able to dry out just about everything. I made my pudding with the milk. Jim and Sue and their son dropped by with a wonderful care package, including cookies, dog treats, a big can of Dinty Moore stew and especially a big box of wooden matches with newspaper in nested Ziplock plastic bags. I used that fire-starting kit the rest of the trip. I saved the stew for hard times. Everything else disappeared before dark. Deb and Morris came back from successfully fishing for walleyes at about 9 p.m. and we all had a nice conversation into the dark. Deb brought me a hot plate of chicken, potatoes, corn and deviled eggs at 10 p.m.–RICHES. They invited me to sleep in their gazebo which I did. Nice hospitality. 10 miles in 7 hours.

#147 The gazebo in Double Bend campground

Monday, June 6. I left about 9 a.m. Took a picture of what I thought was a large hawk in a dead tree, but as it flew off, I could see the white spots of an immature eagle. When they see this photo, many people think the eagle is chasing the small bird, but I am quite sure the smaller bird was harassing the eagle and had just zipped by the eagle's head.

#148 Looks like a big hawk, on CD only

#149 Can see the white spots underneath and broad wings

#150 Dells rapids on the Big Sioux, on CD only

Found 3 exciting rapids verging on scary, with a full canoe, near the town of Dells Rapids. The Dells themselves were impressive–40 feet high rock walls, once on both sides, and thousands of swallows. The current was good but progress was slowed somewhat by the scenery and a south wind which diminished towards evening. Easy portage around 2 three foot dams in Baltic with a 2 hour break, tacos, and Dr. Pepper between portages. Camped at 8 pm. 13 miles.

#151 The Dells of the Big Sioux

#152 Another view, many swallows

Tuesday, June 7. Canoed to the diversion dam in north Sioux Falls. Confusing place with or without a map and I didn't have a map. A friendly young game warden suggested that I go south to avoid a big drop to the east. It wasn't clear to me at the time which fork was the original riverbed as both forks were completely ditched in concrete near the big dam. I followed his advice and am glad I did because this southern ditch became the old river after about 3 miles when it swung east and back north. It flows north for about 2 miles until it goes over the falls and then turns sharply east and then northeast for 3 miles before circling back to the south again, a huge S-curve right in the city and to its east. The eastern route that I didn't take is the high water route which turns south, tumbles down a steep concrete cascade, and dumps into the old riverbed downstream of the falls. I could have gone that way and portaged with my wheels but I would have missed Falls Park and the falls themselves.

I had help from a biker portaging the first big dam so we could slide the canoe without emptying it completely and more help from a hiker at a 2 foot dam further down. A bike trail

#153 Sioux Falls, close up

paralleled my canoe trail the entire distance through the town. The current picked up as the river left the ditch and turned north, including 3 small rapids. I passed through many parks and recreation areas, gaining trees, shade and a volleyball which I sent back with a biker. I pulled into Falls Park when I saw the river disappear ahead of me, tied up my canoe, and hiked the bike path with Daisy on a leash a quarter mile downstream to the falls and found the nightly outdoor sound and light show on the history of Sioux Falls. The falls are still impressive in spite of some idiots taking building granite out of them.

#154 The falls at a distance

The mosquitoes were a bit bothersome but not too bad. After the show and ice cream at the snack bar, we hiked back to the canoe, found an outside receptacle for my cell phone, and set up the tent in basicly downtown Sioux Falls with nary a problem– Hey, this is South Dakota! 13 miles

Wednesday, June 8. Used the bike trail to make 2 trips as usual, crossing the river on the trail bridge. I bought a $4 salad at the snack bar in place of the vitamin pills I wasn't carrying and climbed the tower to get a full view of the falls.

#155 Sioux Falls view from the tower, on CD only

#156 Raccoon down the river some

I commiserated with a kid and his mother about his breaking his fishing line on big carp but couldn't help him. I put the canoe in just below a 2 foot dam still in the park and was whooshed down the river with a nice rapids. I followed the S-curve with good current until it turned south and continued for a few miles to about a mile north of Klondike. I saw a cute, young, dumb raccoon and 13 big owls today; I don't know what kind yet, but they were not horned owls. Cooked Mac and Cheese, cocoa and pudding. 14 miles, but very curvy

Thursday, June 9. Canoed about 9 hours starting at 11 a.m. Had an easy portage at the 4 foot Klondike dam where I talked with a couple on the bridge catching at least one small catfish. A surprise gift of the river was the washed out dam at Canton which was replaced with an easy rapids. I canoed next to a Jim on a punctured plastic raft.

#158 Klondike bridge

#159 Another Jim

I tried to tape the hole but to no avail; he eventually just tied off the leak and blew it up again. I became real tired but enjoyed the scenic float until 8 p.m. and then couldn't find a reasonable campsite. Camped in a wet, smelly cow pasture in the river bottom with lots of mosquitoes. Storm with rain started just as I finished cooking cous-cous with 2 eggs. Ate inside and stayed dry. 20 miles

#160 Pretty Big Sioux

Friday, June 10. I hadn't been sleeping well in spite of being exhausted, until last night. I meant to rise before 7 to be sure to meet Bob Skrukrud and his boys, Carl and Bill, but I slept until 8:40. I skipped breakfast, threw everything into the canoe, and paddled hard to meet them just before the appointment time of noon at the Hawarden bridge. Bob treated us all by staying at the Days Inn and eating at the Mongolian buffet where one picks his raw meat and side dishes which are thrown onto a rotating grill, cooked in front of you.

I had been looking at my South Dakota atlas, wondering if we could find a short cut portage from the Big Sioux over to the Missouri near Elk Point. We found Rosenbaum access (where all 4 boys had a great time setting off fire works) and another boat launch on Mo, but no way of getting off the Big Sioux in spite of nearly getting lost scouting and stuck driving. Did I mention it had been moist? Bob brought me $200 cash for which I exchanged a check. Supper was at KFC. 9 miles in 3 hours

#161 Pyrotechnics with associated maniacs on the river

#162 Wild rose along the riverbank

Saturday, June 11. Started the day with breakfast at the motel with waffles and juice. Bob generously restocked my supplies at Walmart with an air pump, AA batteries, peanut butter, cocoa powder and drink mix, cherry coke, tooth picks, spatula, gloves and dog treats plus tapeworm pills for Daisy. We copied my pictures onto 2 CD's at just $3 each. Bob will send one to Polly so she can put them on the web site and I'll be able to erase some pictures to make room for more. We stopped for lunch in Akron on the way back to the canoe, chicken and French fries. What a wonderful, dry respite, eating better food, cooked by others, for me!

The canoe was still tied up under the bridge and I got on the water by 12:30 and did some hard paddling until 8 p.m. Camped between Akron and Richland on a sand bar. Son Nate had sent to me, via Bob, about 10 nicely sealed packets of precooked East Indian food; I had one for supper, along with one of about 10 large Belgian chocolate bars which he had wedged in between the food packets as packing material, hoping that I "didn't have a craving for Styrofoam peanuts." Oh but they were good! He also sent the camera manual. 15 miles

Sunday, June 12. I called Bob with my newly charged cell phone and found that the new CD stored the photos but not the videos; I never did erase the videos from their 1 gigabyte memory cards. I was passing through north Sioux City towards, evening, thinking of camping when Rick Nearman asked if I wanted a beer, we bargained for a soda, I crashed his daughter Tina's high school graduation party, and stayed the night. Rick's legs were black from pulling my canoe through shore mud so that I could disembark cleanly. I showed my pictures since New Ulm to family and friends, including son Ricky, wife Sara, and her parents. Love flowed in that house; I felt privileged to be taken in. Rick gave me 2 loaves of bread and 6 packages of Raman noodles that night, knowing he'd be gone early next morning to his bakery job. I was invited in but slept outside in my tent. It gently rained about a half inch that night. 14 miles

#163 Tina (in green) and her graduation party

Chapter 8

Me and Mo, First Day

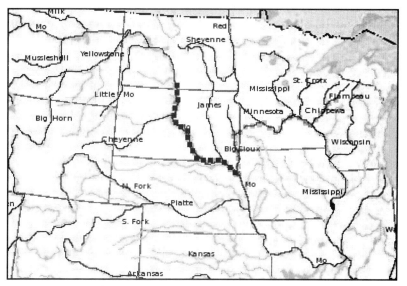

#164 Canoeing The Missouri River in South Dakota

(This chapter is reproduced with some small changes from the story I contributed to my first book.)

My trip in 2005 had a lot of similarities with the Lewis and Clark expedition. I had an almost unlimited amount of time, a lot of my own food, a charge account (credit card in my case) honored at some places, a heavy burden of ignorance but a fair knowledge of canoeing and the outdoors, and a black dog. We

both headed southwest downstream to get to the Mississippi–
Lewis and Clark down the Ohio, I and Daisy down the Chippewa
of Wisconsin. But I joined the Mississippi so much further north
(about 60 miles south of St. Paul, Minnesota) that I decided to
keep that northern latitude as much as possible rather than
canoeing downstream to St. Louis and then upstream back north
to the Dakotas. Thus I canoed (rather slowly, it is true) north up
the Mississippi River to St. Paul, west up the Minnesota through
Mankato to Redwood Falls, west up the Redwood River to Russell,
Minnesota, portaged to Lake Benton and portaged again from
the south end of the lake over Buffalo Ridge to a tributary of the
Big Sioux River, Flandreau Creek. I was in and out of the canoe
down Flandreau Creek into South Dakota and then had a nice
float down the Big Sioux River south through Sioux Falls and to
Sioux City where I turned right up the Missouri River heading
north and west towards Montana.

I had been invited to Tina Nearman's high school graduation
party the evening before, showed them pictures off my camera
onto their TV, and camped in their backyard. Her dad Rick had
made the invitation while I was drifting past, then waded into the
black mud up to his knees to bring my canoe close enough that
I stayed clean. Besides royally
treating Daisy and me, Rick
gave me bread, Ramen
noodles, and other goodies
that evening, knowing he
would be off to his bakery job
before I awoke in the morning.

The next day I had a
pleasant and last 2 mile drift on
the Big Sioux and took pictures
of the Chief War Eagle statue
near the junction. A few
minutes later it was time to
start heading upstream again
as I found the Missouri.

#165 Chief War Eagle monument

114

#166 Junction of the Missouri (left) and the Big Sioux

My first day on big Mo (June 13, exactly 2 months into the trip) was pleasing in that I found I could actually go upstream in spite of the channelization work, especially wing dams, around and above Sioux City. I had to stay close to shore (within 5 feet, closer the better) where the current was less, as I think you can tell from the picture.

#167 Taking a break on Mo

#168 Riprap and rocks on Mo

When I came to a wing dam, it was tempting to let the whirlpool current running along the shore take me up to the wing dam, but then of course the canoe ended up pointed downstream. I tried cutting through the currentless center of the pool, but there was usually a sandbar there where I lost all momentum. What I had to do was to paddle like hell with the canoe positioned just to the shore side of the current coming past the point of the wing dam, keep paddling hard on the shore side to turn the front end just into the current, and hope my 600 pounds of momentum and more paddling would take me far enough up that I could stick a paddle into the rocks on the bottom or shore and push myself past the worst current which is right at the point. When it worked, it took at least 2 pushes and then at least 2 hard paddles to get into the calmer water above, followed by animated panting. Several times I pointed the canoe too much out or missed 1 of the 2 required rock supports and the current would take the front end out and head me back downstream, to try again.

Once I had to pull the canoe up the current while standing on the wing dam; this was not easy either as footing is horrible on the rocks and if the front end had gotten out too far, I'd have had to let it go and hope the safety rope would hold the canoe without tipping it. Success in swimming after the canoe would have depended on the wind direction and my stamina.

On this first day, the river was exciting; I suppose it was about the same size as the Mississippi, but I felt (I think mistakenly) that I knew the Mississippi–I knew little about the Missouri. Where did all that water come from, what kinds of tributaries, what sorts of shores? After about 7 miles of paddling and poddling (poling off the bottom and shore with my sturdy, homemade white ash paddle), and some sailing downwind, upriver, I was invited by Tanner and his father-in-law Bud to spend the night with them. They had been fishing in a slough about 2 wing dams above their docking area and had caught 3 nice catfish. While loathe to go downstream at all, I figured it would be a small effort to come back up the next day compared to the total miles I would be canoeing up the Missouri. I anticipated a safe camp with new friends.

#169 Tanner with catfish

We drifted down to Tanner's beach behind a wing dam, nicely protected. Bud disappeared while I helped Tanner drag his boat up and throw out the anchor. With nothing to tie to, I stuck one of my 10 foot poles into the sand and tied the canoe to it, noting that the pole didn't penetrate the firm sand all that much. I had been able to sail upriver that day, but now it was dead calm. I resolved to drag the canoe up later when I lightened its load. Bud suddenly reappeared with a 4-wheeler, so we threw my backpack, tent pack, and butt pack and myself into the back of the Mule and we all drove about a quarter mile to the house as daylight waned.

Tanner's wife Robin always worked late at the John Morrell meat packing plant, so Tanner fixed us stew. Some friends, most of them named Mike, came to visit so I showed everybody my photos until about 10:30, talked briefly to Robin, and we all went to bed, Daisy and I in the tent in the backyard. 7 miles

#170 Tanner's friends with Bud in center

I was vaguely aware of a storm that night but noted that no or little rain came of it. It was windy when I awoke at about 8, and, having promised sourdough pancakes I walked down to the canoe to get my sourdough starter. But no canoe meant no starter!

The wind had reversed itself from yesterday and was blowing even harder straight downstream. Belatedly, I remembered my intent to drag the canoe up the shore before Bud surprised me with the Mule. I ran back to tell Tanner and he threw a gas can in the Mule, I grabbed my butt pack, and we drove down to the boat. We motored down the left side, Tanner's side, of the river, down river, down wind towards Sioux City. The river was wide open with a current of 6 or 7 mph and wind of something like 20-30 mph. In what seems now like an instant we were pulling into the Mil-R-Tyme Marina without having seen the canoe.

Now what? If the wind came up at midnight 9 hours ago with a current of 6 mph, the canoe could be 50 miles downstream, even without the help of the wind. The longer it might take me to follow, the further down river the canoe would be–what to do, what to do?

The marina was not yet open for business, almost deserted. I was able to fill Tanner's 5 gallon tank using a credit card on the modern gas pump, but he didn't have any oil for the required 2 cycle engine mix. I tried to ask for oil across the water to a raft of docks and boats almost hiding the only movement in the marina. I don't remember the details but 15 minutes later I had given Tanner $10 to buy oil when the Marina opened and was speeding down river at about 30 mph in Tom Garvey's wonderful boat. Tom had come down to check on his boat before an appointment as a tool salesman around noon. We asked people on the way but nobody had seen a wayward canoe, though no one had been in

position since daybreak either. We had a fast, exhilarating trip on the high flat big Missouri all the way down to Decatur, Nebraska without catching that canoe. The Decatur Marina was only half open but I managed to buy $45 worth of gas for Tom with cash; I am sure he missed his appointment.

#171 Tom Garvey

Same question as before, but 40 miles downstream: What to do? I walked the quarter mile to the toll bridge (barefoot, blue jean shorts, T-shirt, thinning hair in the wind), wondering why I hadn't thought of at least sandals but glad I had my cell phone, credit cards and still some cash from writing a check to Bob a few days before. Any trucks going down river? Maybe I could get ahead of the canoe and wait for it to come by! The guys at the toll house were sympathetic and helpful and directed me to the liquor and convenience store across the street where I bought something to eat around 10 a.m. The lady there racked her brain trying to think of someone with a boat not working that day. She called several people to no avail.

I knew I had an ace (well, a prince) in my card hand and finally hatched a plan to play it–I called my younger brother Jon from Colorado who I knew was in Wahoo, Nebraska on business. We had hoped to get together after his work, but maybe now was the time. He dropped everything, was in Decatur by 12:30 and we were in Omaha 60 miles downstream by about 1:30. On the way there, I found and called a couple of marina phone numbers in the Omaha area to see about renting a power boat but no luck. Heading for one of the marinas anyway we found the NP Dodge State Park and boat launch. I walked barefoot on the gravel over to the river to watch for canoes while Jon checked in with the Army Corps of Engineers who had an office there to see if they had any reports or could alert anybody upriver. Jon gave me a pair of sandals and I loitered at the boat launch while he parked his truck. I had left my cell phone number with a few people and found I had a message from Mike, wondering where Tanner was. I called and told him what I knew. Jon and I were discussing how much an airplane ride from the nearby airport to search the river might cost when 2 painters from the area, Kent and Rod, put in Kent's boat to go for a ride on their rainy day off. They liked our story and our offer of $20 per hour plus gas and away we went upriver, with Jon driving his truck up I-29 on the east side of the river to meet us at the Remington boat launch after we found the canoe. No canoe by there so he leapfrogged to the next landing.

Good thing because we were running out of gas by then, fighting the current and the wind. He and Kent found a hardware store to buy 3 five-gallon gas containers, filled them with gas and brought them back to the boat. Kent, Rod and I continued all the way back to the Decatur Marina without finding the canoe. Jon then met us there and Bob and Kirk Hutton let us dock at their marina for free. Jon drove the 2 boaters back to Omaha to get their truck and trailer and bought them gas. I hung around the marina and found I had another message, this one thankfully from Tanner; not only was he OK, but he had found my canoe!

I was able to call Jon and tell the 3 of them the good news while they were trucking down to Omaha. I did my best to call off the canoe watch, calling the Army Corps of Engineers, the toll booth, and through them a message to the police. About 11 pm after Jon, Kent, and Rod had driven their trucks back to Decatur, I took a picture of my pit crew at the marina. The 4 Nebraskans were intrigued by the 1967 "Decatur Marina" sticker I had noticed on Kent's Lone Star boat.

#172 The Search Party in Decatur: (l to r) Rod, Jon, Kent, Kirk, Bob

121

Robin opened up the gate for us around midnight and, after hearing Tanner's story and seeing the canoe, Jon and I slept in Jon's truck. Daisy was fine and lapping up the attention. 0 miles by GPS; 240 miles round trip

Tanner's story: I left Leonard Tanner at the marina in Sioux City at about 9:45 a.m., waiting on the opening which didn't happen until 10:30. After buying the oil and mixing some with the gas, he was on his way home, upriver, upwind. He soon discovered things were awry in Tannerworld. He had no weight in the front of the boat and the wind was so fierce that the front was blown up and around so much that it landed on shore twice, breaking an oar, and probably turning the boat around occasionally. Still he managed to make 5 of the 7 miles before he ran out of gas! Drifting back down he managed to avoid getting caught up in the only tree (a willow) on the far shore, but came close enough to spy my canoe entangled in the branches, still upright. We had missed it as we went downriver on the other side! Of course he couldn't do a thing about it, not even let anybody know he had found it. He managed to beach the boat on a sandy shore, got out and waited 2 hours for help from passing boats. It was such a windy, nasty Tuesday that no one was on the river. What sensation he still had of his legs was pain and his diabetes was probably getting out of control with no breakfast and now no lunch. He clambered back into his boat and, with his one unbroken oar, crossed the mighty Missouri and drifted down to the Riverland subdivision. He struggled out of the boat, crawled up the rocks until he could walk upright with his cane to the house of his friends, got some gas, somehow got back to the boat and was able to start the motor and drive the boat down to the canal and back to the dock of his friends. They gave him a ride home where he called me. Meanwhile his friend Gordy and at least one Mike had called the Jefferson (city) Search and Rescue, knowing Tanner had been out looking for canoes too long.

The Jefferson team didn't find Tanner but they spotted the canoe and towed it back to Tanner's beach with nothing missing but the pole that had been so poorly stuck in the sand. I sent them a $100 check later, but of course they salvaged the rest of my trip along with my canoe– how much was that worth? And what kind of story would this be if Tanner had died out there dealing with my foolish mistakes? I left Ladysmith anticipating new adventure, but explaining myself and apologizing to Tanner's widow and friends was not the type of experiences I had hoped for.

Wednesday, June 15. Penniless Jon left early for Wahoo. (My favorite quote about Nebraska is of Jon's co-worker giving Jon directions to a site before Wahoo: "If you get to Wahoo, you know you've gone too far!") Expecting to see Jon in October, I entrusted him with my shotgun, shells, extra clothes, wool socks, neckpiece.

I cooked sourdough pancakes which nobody but me liked and Robin gave Tanner, Bud and me a ride down to Riverland to retrieve the boat. I took a picture of the willow tree on the uneventful trip back up, and in the early afternoon gave that fat old Vietnam vet a bear hug and took off up the river, wondering what price friendship? 8 miles by river, Mile 745 to 753. 7.5 miles by GPS

#173 The canoe robber

#174 Tanner and Bud bringing their boat back home

Chapter 9

The Unchannelized Missouri

Thursday, June 16. Nebraska's Ponca State Park at mile 752 on the west (Nebraska) side of the river marks the upriver end of wing dams and heavy shore reinforcement, though I encountered a few rock piles, car bodies, and embedded tires further upstream. I had a bit of wind to help me today as I canoed from my camp across from Ponca to across from Volcano Hill, upriver a couple of miles beyond Elk Point. Lewis and Clark mentioned this hill in their journals though at the time I knew nothing about this ancient volcano.

#175 Sailing Mo, on CD only

I rested a bit at Rosenbaum Boat and Fireworks Launch and thought briefly about what might have been if I had portaged from the Big Sioux to there–No graduation party and Nearmans, no Tanner, Bud or Robin, no catfish, Mikes, Tom Garvey, Omaha, speed boats or painters, no bare feet on the gravel, no rescue call for Tanner, no money spent in the race to find a St. Louis bound canoe. Wow. "Won't you please tell the judge I didn't kill any one, I was just trying to have me some fun." John Prine.

I talked to Randy and Pat, drinking beer in their car at a South Dakota boat launch. They knew somebody named Miner upstream who would be especially interested in my trip; they'd tell him to put out a flag for me but I never saw one. 8 miles

Friday, June 17. Canoed from 9 a.m. to 8 p.m. Good tail wind or usable cross wind from 10 to 6. Got water and Pepsi from Lyle, sandwiches, chocolate and 6 blueberry muffins from Joe and Jake who were playing cutthroat gin rummy in Joe's garage. This was near my rest stop about a half mile downstream from the Vermillion River junction. Jake lives in Texas and they winter together on San Padre Island.

#176 Lunch at Joe's place, on CD only

#177 Pretty Mo

#178 Swimming family in wide, sandy Mo

#179 Shorebird "nest"; probably piping plover

The river on this day began channeled, forested, and close but became and remained sandy and wide. The Army Corps of Engineers (ACOE), in charge of the dams and navigation on the Missouri, was trying to protect two bird species, the least tern, a small seagull-like bird with black wing tips, and the piping plover, a killdeer-like bird but with only one black neck ring and a sandy colored back instead of dark brown. I saw several least terns but don't know if I saw piping plovers since I didn't know their distinguishing features from killdeer at the time. They had signs up on the islands especially and even fencing to protect the nesting areas and eggs. I tried to use the Internet to distinguish the eggs of the two species, but both look like the picture here. The number of eggs expected in a least tern nest, however, is 2 with 1 or 3 not unusual; the number of eggs in a piping plover nest is 4 without qualification, so with 4 eggs in the nest pictured, it is probably a piping plover nest. The ACOE were even attempting to vary the flow from the upstream dams so that the birds wouldn't nest in low areas where the eggs would become inundated later; I couldn't quite get their rationale but appreciated their intent.

I hit sand bars about 10 times today. No big deal—I would get out and walk it over if deep enough or sideways until I found a channel. Glad it was nice weather and I wasn't in a hurry. I camped on an island across from Clay County Lakeside Use Area where I could see the bottom of Goat Island upstream. I was orienting myself by comparing my camp GPS latitude and longitude with the DeLorme Atlas and Gazetteer for South Dakota. The numbers in the Atlas were hard to read in camp at night even with my mini-flashlight and reading glasses; in fact I just found an error I had entered into my journal from misreading the GPS, putting in a 3 for a 9. 13 miles

#180 Camp on an island near Vermillion

Saturday, June 18. Had a good tail or cross wind from south or southeast. The river bottom continued wide, with interesting cliffs along the south shore. Two carp shooters in a boat with an elevated stand turned around to talk and gave me a cold bottle of water, the conversation and fluid being a welcomed variation in the day. They were from Sioux City but originally from Canton and Flandreau, so of course interested in my trip. Took a nice lunch break along the sand dunes on the Nebraska side of the river. Camped around the James River delta, a confusing place; never did see the river's entrance; I see now that the James River Island was in the way.

#181 South shore cliffs

#182 Lunch, on CD only

I was learning to sail with tail and cross winds in small waves. One hand on the sheet (rope) that holds the boom against the wind, the other behind me on the square tiller handle leading to the rudder in the back of the boat. Beats paddling, especially against the current, but requires attention. Cross winds are pretty safe because in case a gust of wind comes up that might tip the boat over, you just let the sheet slip; though, loaded as I was, the danger was not in tipping over but in swamping the boat if it tipped too far. Occasionally a little water would come over the leeward gunnel if the gust and a wave timed it just right. I had a big sponge caged inside a mesh tied to a thwart to sponge out such water as well as rain water and especially water that drained off my legs, feet, and shoes if I wore them; I wore out about 5 sponges.

I was pretty well protected so far on the river, but I knew stronger winds and/or longer stretches of water with their bigger waves would be a different matter. Gentle tail winds were wonderful as long as they were enough to overcome the current. I learned even to put my foot on the boom sheet, tie up the tiller or lean backwards into it, and then paddle when the wind faded momentarily. But I could tell that strong tail winds would be tense–I might not be able to hold the sheet against a really strong gust or break something if I could. On the other hand, letting the sheet go entirely (I think that is called "sheet to the wind".) allows the boom and sail to swing forward and removes the resistance to the wind– but then what? You are basicly at the mercy of the wind and waves and better pick up that paddle pretty fast. Besides that, after throwing my particular sheet to the wind, 1) My orange semi-waterproof bag with wheels around it stuck up too far in front for the sail to swing freely. 2) I couldn't reach the hoisting rope to lower the sail. and 3) The boom sheet end was then also out of reach. As I mentioned before, the canoe was too full for me to even crawl towards the front and Daisy was less of a sailor than I.

Strong cross winds will generate some big crossing waves that could easily swamp my overloaded canoe, especially across a quarter mile or more of water like on a big wide reservoir or a narrow reservoir as one crosses a long upwind bay, just as, when driving a van, the wind can rock you as forest gives way to field.

I had some things to work out here and certainly caution was in order. I should also add that the boom extended about a foot past my head to the rear, about temple high; something to watch for when reversing tack or when the wind shifts. 16 miles

Sunday, June 19 Got going by 8:30 a.m., quit at 9 p.m. Wind was again from the south (i.e. a south wind or southerly wind), but I had to paddle or walk the canoe across shallows several times against the wind as the river curved on its way to Yankton. At about 11 a.m. I took a break there to talk with a young father out throwing a net for minnows who happened to catch a sheepshead and then took a stroll into town for Pepsi, bread, candy bars, leaving about $12.

#183 Highway 81 bridge near Yankton, South Dakota

On the way to the Gavins Point Dam, I saw my first paddlefish of the trip. I knew what it was from seeing one in the southern USA; it was pretty clear that a motorboat propeller had killed this one, just like the one in Tennessee. Paddlefish are plankton eaters that haven't changed much in millions of years; they can get up to 80 pounds and are only caught by snagging when they are more concentrated during their spawning run. (More on them later.)

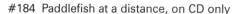

#184 Paddlefish at a distance, on CD only

#185 Paddlefish, close up

131

#186 Gavins Point dam, holding back Lewis and Clark Lake

As I came in view of the dam, a family was boating in the channel leading up to the dam and the father, an employee of the Corps, helped me lift and drag the canoe and carry the baggage up the steep, rocky, 30 feet of shore. Then I did my usual 2 carries up and over the dam to an easy putin all within a half mile. Made good progress on flat Lewis and Clark Lake. Impressive cliffs on south shore noted by Lewis and Clark. Rocky steep sides developed on the north shore also, and I was happy to find a tent size opening. 13 miles

#187 Helpful family

#188 South shore cliffs

#189 Camp

Monday, June 20. Got up at 6 a.m. to a stiff wind from the southwest or west, but my windup radio said that it should be southerly. The wind died by the time I got going, probably a good thing, a big, placid lake. The cliffs continued on both sides of the lake.

#190 Impressive rock

#191 Pretty shoreline on a placid lake, on CD only

About the only thing I asked for on my trip (besides information and advice) was water, though I here shamelessly admit that occasionally I asked for it in solid form. The highlight of the day might be a cold soda pop with my peanut butter and bread, pancake, or fry bread. I preferred water over warm pop. A kind fisherman gave me a half bag of ice that day. I suppose on the Internet somewhere I could look up the temperature that day, but let's just say it was hot.

INTERNET REALITY CHECK: Only 85 degrees in Yankton, you wimp.

The Atlas makes it look like Lewis and Clark Lake extends right up to Springfield, but because this and most upstream reservoirs were low, there was some current to overcome on the way to their boat launch and nice park.

#192 Good beaver habitat, on CD only

#193 Springfield park, looking at the cliffs I passed, on CD only

#194 Nice fish, friendly people

I talked to Nancy and her husband as they were cleaning fish. They said fishing used to be better and the water deeper around there. Did a little shopping in Springfield, friendly people. Talked to Tanner by cell phone.

As I left Springfield I knew I needed to follow current in this wide, flat, weedy area, but when the current passes through a quarter mile wide pond, there is not much to follow and occasionally some flow comes through impenetrable swamp. I had to back track twice out of half mile dead-ends including one late in the evening that had me canoeing almost in a panic. I was happy to find dry land on the north edge of the swamp near a road about 3 miles southwest of Springfield. There was not even tent space along the gravel road so I moved up the fairly fast current and camped across the current and the road on the small Curt Memorial plot of grassy ground. I knew nothing about Curt or Mr. Curt but I treated that plot with reverence and extreme gratitude. I was tired from escaping the swamp in daylight. I saw perhaps the best sunset of the whole trip. I heard thunder from the south as I went to sleep. 9 miles

#195 Sunset in the swamp

Tuesday, June 21. Wind came up about midnight. It flattened the dome tent, breaking one tent pole in 2 places. No big deal, I was still warm and dry. An hour later it started raining. It rained hard and the wind blew even stronger than before. I admit it, I was an unhappy camper, totally wet and a little cold already. It had been way too hot to be in a sleeping bag, so I was in skimpy underwear, holding on to tent-like material with both hands because I didn't know which hand, if either, had the fly which would probably fly into the current if I let go, in the dark, the wet, the wind, the cold. The lightening was awesome through the tent material and through my eyelids. I wanted to inspect and perhaps fix the tent, but with the current 10 feet downwind I was afraid of losing things just from shifting my weight. And the wind blew. And blew strong. For 2 hours.

INTERNET REALITY CHECK: Yankton registered a maximum wind gust speed of only 44 mph at 5:30 a.m., later than my maximum around 2 a.m.; besides, the storm came from the south and I think the main wind missed Yankton, 30 miles to the east.

Finally the wind and rain lessened enough that I slithered out, separated and secured the fly, found my duct tape and repaired the tent pole which collapsed immediately. I slithered back into the tent, into the sleeping bag which was not yet totally wet and spent the next 3 hours until dawn at 5:30 laying on my side in the same uncomfortable but not cold position.

I had secured the canoe well to an iron stake given to me by Tanner. There was an inch of rain in the dog dish. Daisy had fared much better than I, just by curling up in the weeds somewhere. I threw everything into the canoe, paddled hard up the current and managed to find Niobrara State Park on the Nebraska side about 3 miles up.

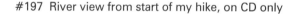

#196 Highway 37 bridge at Running Water, SD, on CD only

I dried things out for about 3 hours during which time I walked up the Niobrara Trail as far as the bridge over the Niobrara. I felt lucky that I hadn't lost anything the night before and everything looked better bathed in sunshine rather than lightening. As I left the park, I had to retreat from another half mile dead-end in my attempt to find the main river course. I had water in my left ear all day. I camped in a field on the South Dakota side and took a hike into pretty cedars and hills, seeing deer and turkey. 9 miles

#197 River view from start of my hike, on CD only

#198 Deer amidst the cedars and meadows

#199 Turkey in the dead trees, center

Wednesday, June 22. I paddled for about an hour and then caught a southeast wind as I was going northwest. Scenery was entertaining. Sometimes I had to paddle as the wind would die, but it kept coming back. Took a lunch break on the Nebraska side and climbed a hill, apparently the last hill for a while.

#200 Intriguing gully

#202 View from the last of the cliffs, on CD only

#203 Steep cliffs, small canoe

Towards evening I carried my sleeping and cooking equipment onto a sand bar towards the South Dakota side, but I was flooded out as I cooked supper, so moved to the highest spot on the bar, to the right in the picture, leaving the canoe tied to a snag in the sand. During the day I had seen a bald eagle, least terns, gulls, nighthawks, crows, and vultures. At evening I heard whipperwills, bobwhite quail, and bull frogs. 22 miles, mostly sailing.

#204 Initial camp site

Thursday, June 23. The tent I was now using was wet inside after the night before when set up in the grass; it was reasonably dry this morning on the open sand bar. There wasn't room inside to fully extend the thermarest even diagonally but just enough room for me at 6 foot one inch. When I awoke the canoe was where I tied it but 135 yards from any water!

#206 The ups and downs of river camping

I had several opportunities to count the yards as I dragged the empty canoe and carried the baggage to the current through ankle deep mud. Took about an hour for the mud portage. For breakfast I had the last of the Springfield Cheerios and milk. Last night I saw the lights of Pickstown, right next to the Fort Randall Dam holding back Lake Francis Case. As I sailed this morning, I could see it for 2 hours before reaching it at 11 a.m.

#207 Scenery up to Fort Randall Dam

There was no water at all coming out of the dam or power house, so I couldn't canoe to the boat launch, demanding 20 yard carries to the tarmac. Then about a 2 mile portage twice on the south side to the first picnic area on the lake. Don and Karen Tiede from Sioux City gave me a Pepsi and offered to check on Daisy who was tied up in the shade near the takeout. They grew up watching the dam being built. The brand new Pickstown school psychologist was sun bathing at the picnic area. She gave me a gallon of water and a map of the lake. Hottest day of the year I was told. Tough carries up the hill, middle of the day. Daisy was fine and hightailed it to the water ASAP. 15 miles, sailing.

INTERNET REALITY CHECK: high temperature was 91 degrees in Lake Andes, close by

#208 Hot day, interesting view

#210 Lake Francis Case, easy paddling, on CD only

#211 Pretty bay at putin

Friday, June 24.   Sailed 9 hours, 9:30 to 6:30 to Dock 44 Marina. I took a survey as I canoed past 10 fishing boats on the north side of the lake: only 5 walleye, 15 inch minimum.

#212 Sample walleye, friendly fishermen, on CD only

At Dock 44 I bought my South Dakota fishing license for $62. Also bought a nice lunch of hamburger and chicken wings with the bones for Daisy. The owner, Kevin, gave me his personal fly swatter as the store was out of them. The biting, house-fly size black flies would find us out in the middle of the lake, sometimes swarms of them; they were driving Daisy nuts and making me put on socks to cover my bare ankles and toes. Life improved with that swatter–Daisy would snap at them until they came my way, then I'd put the boom sheet in my teeth or under my foot, kill the little suckers as they often landed on the white sail, and feed them to the lake.

Overcast most of the day with wind from behind all day. I paddled out of the bay and then sailed another hour after the marina. Tired, especially my back. 38 river miles, 32 miles GPS

Saturday, June 25. I was on the water from 8 a.m. until 6:30 p.m. I was trying to meet friends from Ladysmith, Kevin Smith and his 4 boys, where they would be camping tomorrow in Chamberlain, but it looked pretty hopeless yesterday morning. I was then about 60 straight line miles from Chamberlain and had

#213 Sailing a green shoreline

at most 3 days to get there, 20 miles a day. I had averaged 15 GPS miles per day over the last 6 days. But that strong east wind yesterday allowed me to make 32 miles and 27 miles today by about 6 p.m.

I was looking forward to a Cedar Shores Resort and Campground shower when I turned the last corner, viewed the city to the northeast, faced that wonderful wind head on, took a half hour to go a quarter mile and could go no further. (If you remember Jim's wind rankings, this would be an RPO.) I backed up to the south shore and camped close to the city of Oacoma, taking a hike to the convenience store in the distance. I am trying to make a smug comment about how other people have to buy gasoline from such stores, but I can't think of a way to do it with any respectable amount of humor.

I was sleeping in the open listening to the roar of the wind until it quit at about 2 a.m. allowing the mosquitoes to attack. I set up the tent then and brought Daisy and my back pack in when it started raining a little at 4. I had been treating Daisy monthly with Frontline which kills ticks and fleas after they have sucked enough blood and chemical. After I picked 10 ticks off of me that had evidently crawled off their black furry host, I showed Daisy the door. There was an obnoxious animalistic cluck sound every 3 seconds around dawn; turned out to be a yellow-headed blackbird. 27 miles

Sunday, June 26. I awoke to a stiff southeast wind and had to go almost east to get around the railroad, I-90, and Highway 50 bridges, so tacked into the wind with hard paddling besides for about an hour to make the corner and then sailed into Cedar Shores about 10:30 a.m. I paid $10.80 for slip #38A overnight and washed and dried clothes while waiting for my friends. I was down to 70 cents in cash. Had a nice shower. Kevin and kids, along with Kevin's brother Gregg and his wife Martha arrived at 1:30, all on their way to the Black Hills. We lazed away the day eating, swimming, talking.

#214 Ian, Joe, Elliot, Kevin, Jon

Elliot got a kick out of shaving my hair and beard with an electric barber shears I had asked Kevin to bring, after which I shaved. I felt light-headed and clean. We had supper in their RV and I made pudding. 2 miles

Monday, June 27. Kevin bought us breakfast at the resort restaurant and his kids helped me pack the canoe and saw me off about 12:30. I paddled upwind and upcurrent on way to Big Bend dam and Lake Sharpe. Caught a 14 inch small mouth bass in the clear water below the dam, my first fish. Also saw my first cormorant nests in a pretty area of South Dakota. 13 miles

#215 Leaving Chamberlain

#216 Cormorants with nests

#217 Nice scenery, on CD only

#218 Nice day

Tuesday, June 28. Today was a day of new people. But first I had bass for breakfast. Then I evidently canoed about 3 miles up to the end of Lake Francis Case, and portaged the Big Bend dam into Lake Sharpe, though I have no notes or memory of doing so; or rather I can force a memory but I'd bet 6 to 1 that it is wrong, the number of dams portaged here in the west being about 6. I found that if I didn't put a note in my journal the following day at the latest, that day was basicly lost or the memorable parts of that day were filed with other such memories and were perhaps pleasant but pretty useless.

I met Jeff Otten on his way from Gardiner, Montana, to St. Louis, rowing a double-hulled inflatable kayak. He mentioned 6 diversion dams on the Yellowstone to watch out for if I ever made it that far which almost sounded like a bad joke. For weather reasons he spent considerable time at the other end of Lake Oahe and recommended I stop and see Eric at the Mobridge library.

#219 Jeff Otten

It was a pleasant day, but hot (Internet says max of 87, min of 63) and when a boat stopped by to talk, I innocently asked if they had a cup of ice to garnish my soda pop for lunch. I assumed anyone that could afford a boat and a day on the water would have a whole chest full of ice. But no, they didn't. But they evidently raced back to their dock, bought at least one bag of ice, caught up to me a half hour later, and gave me one!

#220 Ice givers

An hour later I met Andrew Marsters rowing his way backwards from Billings, Montana, to St. Louis. He was a recent graduate of a Washington art college. (Read more in the book I edited, We Were on the Missouri, 2005, published by Author House.) I shared some ice from my highly successful begging along with a Pepsi, and Andrew gave me a book, 1984. He had wheels for his craft also and had portaged Big Bend just ahead of me. His complaints on wind and weather sounded eerily similar

#221 Andrew Marsters

to those of Jeff. With an uncanny and damn slow cleverness I finally realized that the same easterly wind that propelled me 60 miles in 2 days had held them wind bound for days, enough to apparently wound a sensitive lad like Andrew for life. (See my introduction to his story for more smart-ass comments.)

> MORE ON WIND DIRECTION: From Bruce Watson showing "wind roses" in the 2002 Minnesota Weatherguide, data from the weather in Roseville, Minnesota during the year 2000: A short summary on wind direction would be 1) Much more often from the North and Northwest from November through March. 2) Much more often from the South and Southeast from June through September. 3) Undecided in April, May and October. This same summary applied also to his data of year 2006. MORAL: Go west in the summer!

Following Andrew's hints at directions and a helpful finger from a reservation kid (I was on the Lower Brule Indian Reservation.), I found a road out of a Powwow parking lot that became a trail with Andrew's wheel marks still visible leading across the 3/4 mile Narrows of the Big Bend, which would cut off about 19 miles of Lake Sharpe. The western drop down to the lake was pretty rough and a little long so I opted out of the portage, figuring that it would take a day either way.

If I really was clever, I might have reasoned that if there were any strong wind during this one day trip, by traveling in a 19 mile circle I would certainly come up against it at some time. But I wasn't clever and didn't so reason.

On my hike across the Narrows, I happened to meet Lynn and Doug Davis literally walking in the footsteps of Lewis and Clark who also investigated the Narrows back in 1804. (See the Davis's story also in my first book.) We camped and ate together in their camper back at the lake and I made pudding. Nice folk. 14 miles

#222 Doug and Lynn Davis

Wednesday, June 29. I had breakfast with the Davises and got a good start on Big Bend, heading north and a little northwest but sheltered from the westerly wind by the peninsula. When I got to the northern point of Big Bend, I became windbound for the rest of the day by a horrendous northwestern wind and waves that would come over ends and sides of my loaded canoe no matter which way the canoe faced.

#223 Pelicans on Lake Sharpe, on CD only

#224 RPO wind

No big deal, I'll just hike and enjoy the scenery; unfortunately there wasn't any. I did hike but all I found was completely flat land and irrigation circles growing barley, soybeans, chick peas, and corn, connected by brush. Back in camp I tried to read 1984, but, having read it years ago, found it more boring than staring at the waves. The wind was so strong I couldn't fish. I hiked a little again and welcomed darkness as an excuse to sleep. 5 miles

Thursday, June 30. My hopes rose at midnight but were dashed by dawn. My answer to this was a longer hike, almost back to the Narrows (about 3 miles), where there were a few hills. On the way back I nearly encountered sensory overload as Daisy found a badger at the same time that the reservation caretaker drove up in his pickup.

#225 Daisy and badger

I got a poor picture of the badger but a nice talk with the caretaker, a non-Indian. He said there was a herd of 5 antelope which I might have seen at a distance, thinking they were mule deer. He also mentioned rattlesnakes which got my attention. I did find a snake skin shed about 7 feet long (not a rattler) which I kept. I was checking the waves all day and finally convinced myself at 5 p.m. that maybe I could leave. So I loaded up the canoe without Daisy, hoping the front end would be high enough which it was, but water came in near me in the back. I went back to shore, dragged the canoe up and out of danger, emptied the water with bucket and sponge, and tried a new tactic. I waded out about a quarter mile with the canoe pointed into the waves until the water was waist high but the waves weren't always breaking and then pushed the canoe sideways, side-wind, with the boat always perpendicular to the waves. It took about a half hour to walk the half mile past the north point where I managed to find some calmer water, helped Daisy in, jumped in myself, raised the sail, and sailed an easy 4 miles until 9:30 p.m. where I found a somewhat muddy sand bar between the willow and the river across from the Narrows. 5 wonderful miles

Friday, July 1. Completely calm. Radio implied wind from the south today, but I paddled into a weak west wind for 3 hours until it shifted to the south, and then to the east. My notes don't say whether the wind was strong enough for sailing, but usually if there was any tail wind (I was going west quite often.) I would use it and paddle besides if needed, especially on a lake; a river with current against me required a pretty good minimum wind behind me. My picture of a young cormorant shows the sail out using a cross wind.

#226 Young cormorant; I should have tried fishing

#227 Two deer on the prairie, on CD only

I could see fireworks in Pierre from my hike into the hills where I saw about 5 mule deer. I could also see lightening further to the west, but no storms on me this night. 29 miles, so I must have sailed a lot!

Saturday, July 2. I gave Daisy 2 more tapeworm pills and squirted a monthly dose of Frontline on her back. Arose to a nice east wind that should blow me the 7 miles into Pierre today. But the wind rotated to the south and then west right against me. I ran out of Lake Sharpe early on today and was paddling against current too. My Atlas helped me avoid the 3 mile long bay on the north side of Farm Island, which is apparently a peninsula, not an island. The next fork to the right seemed well used, though with no current it had to be a dead end. Actually such possibilities are not that much of a gamble because one doesn't invest much energy in them, easy in, easy out–just make sure the out part doesn't happen in the dark in a swamp. This dead-end rewarded me with free camping at Griffin Park in downtown Pierre. Plus when I wanted to continue, I wouldn't even have to backtrack and then fight current to come back–just portage a hundred foot wide low dam to a boat launch on the main river using my wheels. I couldn't see that on the Atlas before I got there and I still can't see it as I write this.

I went grocery shopping 3 blocks away on Sioux Avenue and spent $40; walked right past the capital. Got a replacement tent pole kit from the DakotaMart, but had to settle for a millimeter bigger set of poles as they didn't have the 8 millimeter size. I made it work but it was a sloppy fit. Nice time to relax and pig out on food and drink. Met a friendly family that came to play in the water. I got directions to the local WalMart for picture transfer, but then they cell-phoned the family patriarch, Bud Hall, who took me over there in his truck. Bud has a wonderful story in my book of stories.

#228 The capital of South Dakota in Pierre, rhymes with deer

Fellow campers with RVs advised those of us with tents that a big evening wind was coming. I postponed tent erection and pulled up and tied off my canoe. All evening there was a stiff east wind blowing. About midnight the wind just stopped, followed by at most 5 minutes of dead calm, followed by a predicted 50 mph wind with dust from the west. Native American families near me rode it out even as their tents partially collapsed, betting that their weight would keep the tents from flying off. A little rain collected most of us in the bath room overhang, but calm followed as I set up my tent. 11 miles

REALITY CHECK: I am not writing this the day after the storm and I don't need to restrict myself to hearsay from an unknown RV owner. I am writing this in December, 2007, and I have access to weather information through the Internet at wunderground.com. Here are the actual wind speeds registered at the Pierre airport:

DATE	TIME	WIND DIR.	WIND SPEED	GUST SPEED
July 2, 2005				
	10:52 pm	ESE	10 mph	15 mph
	11:39 pm	Variable	10	—
	11:47 pm	NW	35.7	62.1
	11:48 pm	NW	38	62.1
July 3, 2005				
	12:00 am	N	32.2	44.9
	12:34 am	N	21.9	27.6

How about the days I was stranded on Big Bend? Again as registered at the Pierre airport:

June 29, 2005			
	afternoon	more than 20, ave 30	44.9 mph
June 30, 2005			
	afternoon	more than 15, ave 20	27.6

How about the day I lost my canoe and the next day's wind that threw Tanner around until he was out of gas? Sioux City airport:

June 13, 2005				
	5:52 pm	S	11.5mph	—
(Bye-bye canoe)				
	11:52 pm	NW	19.6	25.3 mph
June 14, 2005				
	12:52 am	NW	17.3	27.6
(Tannerworld awry)				
	2:52 pm	NW	26.5	35.7

Holy Smokes, Folks! If you like fizz in your soda,
you'll like the weather in South Dakota!

Sunday, July 3. So the wind really did change last night, from 10-15 mph from the east southeast to 36 to 62 mph from the northwest. I didn't feel like making 2 portages in one day, and kind of wanted to see the Independence Day fireworks, so I took my time drying the tent, packing the canoe, and making phone calls with my newly charged cell phone, good phone service in Pierre, and free calls on a Sunday. Reconda of the tent people offered me a large portion of their breakfast of eggs, potatoes, carrots, bacon which I snapped up with thanks and then shared with another itinerant who admitted he was hungry and looking for work. I had cereal and milk also, always a treat. Close to noon I canoed to the causeway and made the easy portage while Daisy lapped up attention from some bathing beauties waiting for a boat ride to a beach party.

#230 Pierre pretties

I had a hard upwind paddle past the bridges and then turned east to shallow water and walked the canoe past the party beach and onto the south tip of an apparent island where I camped on a sand bar and tried fishing without luck. Saw a few fireworks that night. Counted 30 mosquitoes on the outside of my entry netting. 3 miles

Monday, July 4. Absolutely clear and cold water coming out of the Oahe Dam. Trolled with a Rapala on way to dam and caught 12, 13, and 14 inch smallies, all released as I didn't want to deal with fish today. There were no size restrictions on bass, limit of 5. I kept left into a dead-end lagoon but got within 10 feet of smooth concrete for my wheels. Evan gave me a car tour (and minnows) to scout out my route from there. Took 3 hours to twice portage the 2 miles to a boat launch on Lake Oahe, also on the south side. As I paddled out of the boat launch, I found that people were catching walleyes all over and trying for salmon near the dam in 120 feet of water. I just canoed to a protected area somewhat out of the north wind where I met the Olson family. Blaine was a federal parole officer in Pierre. They gave me nightcrawlers, candy, sinkers, ice and a map. I tried a half hour of fishing out of a bobbing canoe with a moving stone anchor, but it was too stressful in the rough waves, and unproductive. Later when it calmed down, I caught a nice catfish and just missed a walleye of about 20 inches. 4 miles

#231 Nice walleye

#232 Blaine, Susan, Maddison, Kayla

Tuesday, July 5. Had catfish for breakfast, with a start on using the 5 boxes of Shore Lunch coating I had brought 500 miles from home for the occasion. Had a usable wind, all day I think. Hiked once midday and then again at camp, close to Mail Shack Creek. Caught 2 smaller catfish late in the evening when I didn't want to clean them, so built a little enclosure of rocks in the water to keep them. Also caught a goldeye shad (a flat bony fish) and a sheepshead. Only one tree around for firewood. 18 miles

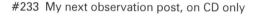

#233 My next observation post, on CD only

#234 Where I came from

#235 View to the east, Mailshack Creek, on CD only

#236 Where I am going, on CD only

Wednesday, July 6. The shale that I used to enclose the catfish dissolved away overnight; sometimes in shallow water near shore I sank to my ankles in weak shale. Jailbreak allowed a quicker getaway for me also as it shortened breakfast to probably oatmeal and I was off to a 7 a.m. start with a good wind towards Little Bend.

But same deal as at Big Bend–going in a circle can turn a good wind bad. When it came time to sail cross wind, the waves were too big and one broke over the gunnel on the right side, offering about 20 refreshing gallons. I knew we could carry the extra 160 pounds; the problem would be the next 30 gallons from being now lower in the water. I was a mile from any shore, even the down wind shore which would have ended the day wind-bound and wet with water coming over the stern as I unloaded. Unlike Big Bend, this was not waist-deep water causing the waves to break, this was middle of the lake deep. I wouldn't have known what to do a month ago, but I knew now–Let the boom swing but hang on to the end under my foot, PICK UP THE PADDLE, paddle on the left, get some speed, backwater on the right to turn into the wind and waves, paddle as needed to keep it there while I lower the sail, toss the minnows, bail the water (My end of the canoe was heaviest so the water always came to me.), keep paddling upwind, keep bailing as the water came over the bow, drenching Daisy–STAY!, paddle for a half hour until you get to calm water–GOOD DOG!.

I think it was all paddling after that. I noticed a lot of boats that seemed to keep trolling in the same muddy, wind-agitated water and found that they were catching fish. So I tried it myself,

#237 Great fishing--perch (top), walleye, catfish

nightcrawlers on the bottom, and caught a 21.5 and 18 inch catfish, a 14 inch walleye, a nice perch, a large sheepshead, and a 20 inch sucker, as measured with the ruler taped to the inside of the boat. There was no minimum size on walleye/sauger, limit 6, no more than 4 over 14 inches, no more than 1 over 20 inches. Got that? No size or daily limit on catfish. I ate fish that day and the next. The Cheyenne River and Reservation were on the west but I never saw the river. 9 miles GPS but included Little Bend; with my rolling map wheel on the Atlas here at home, it was 21 miles.

Thursday, July 7. Hardly any notes and certainly don't remember. I see in my pictures that I must have caught a goldeye around lunch time; lunch looked like minute rice, dried veggies, and some fish from last night. Also from pictures, it looks like I had some wind with me and at camp time, I fished and took pictures of what I called the "water walker" plant; the seeds from this plant had long slender, stiff stalks that would allow the seed to tumble across the water for miles with a good wind.

#238 Goldeye and lunch

#239 Livestock on typical shore

#240 Waterwalker plant

#241 Waterwalker seeds, close up

From my notes, I camped in a shallow bay, 2-3 feet deep where I caught a carp with a nightcrawler. While I was casting a perch Rapala along the rocky shore upstream in view of the Highway 212 bridge, I had a hit but lost it. Nice sunset. 19 miles

#242 Highway 212 bridge near Gettysburg, SD

#243 Sunset, on CD only

Friday, July 8. Got up at 5:40 a.m. Paddled against an east wind to the bridge (3 miles), then sailed cross wind for a mile until the wind died. So fished and caught a 14 inch walleye and 16 inch catfish in about 12 feet of water, drifting into shore. I don't have a lot of notes on meals, so I'll relate my notes for the day: Leftover sourdough pancakes with my home-made maple syrup for breakfast, more such pancakes with peanut butter and water for lunch, fish and 3 eggs for late lunch, pecans and Kool-Aid for supper. I bought eggs pretty often for my chocolate

#244 Where I came from

161

tapioca pudding especially; but I found they were a great stand-bye for tweaking cous cous, fish, pancakes, or most anything as I never had one go bad even in this heat. I found algae growing well in my last gallon of water but wasn't about to toss it; I never got sick the whole trip.

#245 Where I am going, on CD only

Sailed a lot as a gentle tail wind came up, kept at it until 7 p.m. Back pain.

Took a hike to a nearby butte. As I walked on the ridge overlooking the lake I saw a badger hole; 20 feet further a scared rattlesnake, maybe 30 inches long, went hissing, rattling and writhing into another hole. Got my attention. Saw the lights of the town of Mobridge, South Dakota. 27 miles

#246 Badger hole containing scared rattlesnake, on CD only

Saturday, July 9. Had good wind again after 2 miles of paddling upwind and sailed close to Mobridge; tough walk through brush into town, over a mile. Parked the canoe near an outdoor movie screen. I copied the journal covering from New Ulm to here and made 2 CD of pictures, sending all to Polly. Bought cold orange juice, chocolate milk, 2 pounds cookies, bananas, 4 lemon Bismarcks. I visited the Klein Museum which had a good collection of books by Missouri River travelers; rest of collection overwhelming. Slow hike back to canoe with heavy groceries. Crossed the lake to Grand River Campground in high waves but with the wind. This was a really nice, tribally run campground with shade trees, showers, bathrooms, electricity, and hundreds of sites. $15 regular, only $8 for this senior citizen over 55. I portaged everything to my site. I must have looked needy; a boating family sent their little girl over to give me $2; Terry, a camper from Michigan gave me $5; somebody left chewy treats for Daisy on the picnic table. All appreciated, a nice social break. 14 miles

162

Sunday, July 10 On my way out of the campground boat launch I met fishermen coming in with their limit of 6 walleyes, 14-16 inches. They knew of an inundated former island now of depth 25 feet where rest of lake was 50 feet or more. About 5 miles upstream I found an upside-down 14 foot aluminum boat which I cleaned up and tried to tow as I sailed but it towed poorly. I tied it to a log and reported its position to the South Dakota Game, Fish and Parks Department when I found phone service; they said they would pick it up.

I sailed with a south wind that died at camp time, but with a storm brewing in the west. There was a 3 foot bank on the west side, so I couldn't drag the canoe out of the water without emptying it. I tied it to a log figuring that the bank would shelter the canoe from a western wind. Maybe so, but wind came from the north and swamped the canoe before I realized it around midnight. I jumped into the crashing waves, threw stuff onto the bank, and lifted the canoe out of further danger. 15 miles

Monday, July 11. That morning I found that I had lost the top to the pot from my cooking kit, a T-shirt, my beloved fly swatter, and $80 worth of Atlases–SD, ND, MT, and WY. (I had left WI at home and MN in Lake Benton.) Bummer. The maps were in a waterproof plastic envelope so I searched the west shore to the south on foot for a mile with no luck. The wind continued to rage from the north, so I did what any good frontiersman would do–I took a long nap. Then, with a lot less wind and an empty canoe, I paddled about a quarter mile out to one of many snags, tied up and caught all the catfish I could want in a half hour. I kept 4, the biggest one being 22 inches. I cooked them for supper and for the next day. The wind died down by 8 p.m. I vowed to get an early start manana. 0 miles

#247 Surrounding area, on CD only

#248 Camp and windy lake

#249 Catfish haven, windless next day

#250 Nightcrawler box with catfish; pliers for hook removal and skinning

Tuesday, July 12. Up at dawn. Had Cheerios with skim milk from powder (another staple) for breakfast, peanut butter and bread for lunch, and catfish for supper, probably with minute rice. First did a 10 mile cruise looking for maps along both shores with no luck. Continuing on, I paddled against a weak north wind, then calm most of the day, but with a mild tail wind in the evening. With the reservoir down 30 feet, I was paddling through a dead forest. Found another boat, a jon boat (not pointed at either end) from Wisconsin; I didn't report it as I thought I might be able to pick it up on my return trip. I tried to contact the owner in Wisconsin but couldn't find a current address or phone number. It might still be there, but I doubt it. I camped on a sand bar, away from the muddy shore. First camp in North Dakota, not that you could tell from the scenery. 19 miles.

#251 Sometimes underwater here

#252 Second boat; could be a sad story behind this

Chapter 10

North Dakota Mo

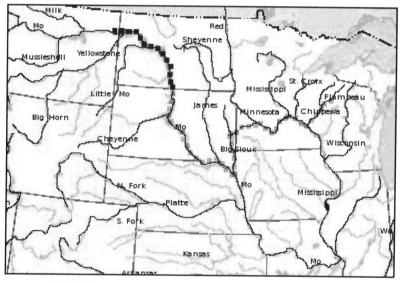

#253 Canoeing the Missouri River through North Dakota

Wednesday, July 13. Three months of trip! I was 456 miles from home on a direct line and 938 miles by the camp-to-camp addition of GPS miles at my first overnight in North Dakota. This was truly becoming an interstate adventure.

Away by 7:30 a.m. Had a brisk south tail wind, always on the edge of being too much. Stopped at Fort Yates and had the $6 goulash at the Missouri Drift Inn where I met Ben Potter and Troy, electricians working on some temporary project. I stopped at a gas station and got a free North Dakota Highway map, then shopped at the only, small grocery store for eggs, bread, 2 pounds of grapes (from Chile probably!) and gloves. Clerks generously directed me to where I could fill my 4 gallon milk jugs with water. Nice people, Indians and whites living together well it seemed. Fort Yates is the headquarters for the huge Standing Rock Reservation, which borders the Cheyenne River Res to the south. Difficult, but short walk (quarter mile) back to canoe with 32 pounds of water plus groceries. Still had one gallon in canoe.

On the river I met Mike Moont and his son Shane from Lakewood, Colorado, on their trip from Three Forks, Montana, to I-don't-recall. I also don't remember what kind of boat they had, but they had arranged for rides to bypass the 2 big lakes ahead of me, Sakakewea in North Dakota, and Fort Peck in Montana. I wondered why.

There was a stiff current around and above Fort Yates, the river being only about 200 yards wide. From the ND Atlas you would think there would be a lot of lake left but the Oahe reservoir was down about 30 feet. At an average river drop of 1 foot per mile, this would imply an extra 30 miles of current for me. Looking at the Atlas now, it measures out to more like 40 mile from Fort Yates to the top of the "normal" lake boundary. I use the quotation marks because the lakes have been down for years and seem to be shrinking still. Without much help from the wind, I paddled until 8 p.m. 15 miles

REALITY CHECK: According to my Internet sources, Lake Oahe continued to drop after my visit, hitting an all time low of 32 feet down from normal on August 30, 2006. The lake level has been coming back up, to only 23 feet down a year later, August 28, 2007. Well, good, I was wrong.

Wednesday, July 14. Had a stiff east wind to start with and made good progress sailing north and northwest, but it faded after an hour and a half. So poddled and poled and then roped, i.e. cordeled. My cordeling technique evolved like my sailing and portaging techniques, but faster.

Pulling a rope tied to the front of a craft works well if you are wading in deep enough water (Around ten men with a big rope pulled Lewis and Clark and their keelboat in this manner.) or have 2 ropes and 2 people on opposite sides to cancel sideways forces. But how about 1 guy who wants to stay on shore or in water lower than his boot tops?

Trying to canoe up the Gunnison River in Colorado years ago, brother Jon and I discovered that one guy could pull the canoe by tying to the front seat or the thwart near it, but needed the other guy in the canoe to keep it the proper distance out and parallel to shore by steering with his paddle. As near as I can tell, this is basicly how boats were towed on the Erie and other canals--A boy drove a mule or two on the bank and the captain on the rudder kept the barge from bumping land; the one picture I saw even showed the rope being tied not to the front of the boat, but to a sturdy post towards the front in the middle. But, back to the one man situation, is there a sweet spot to tie to on the canoe so that the canoe would trail you at a fixed distance from shore? The answer is superficially "yes" but the real world answer is "no" because the spot changes with about 6 main factors–speed and direction of the current and of the wind, walking speed, and depth of canoe in the water.

Let's consider the difference between a slow section of a river and a rapids. You are walking the calmer area after finding the sweet spot for all the factors above, just by moving attachment point of the 25 feet of rope. Why isn't the canoe coming in to shore? Because the attachment point is back of the prow by about 5 feet near the front seat, pulling that part of the canoe towards you on shore. The part of the canoe towards the front is thus at an angle to the direction of movement, finds less friction to the water as it moves mid-river, and is thus always pushing the canoe away from shore (the rest of the canoe seems to just follow the front's lead), balancing the rope pull towards shore just as if you had a partner pulling from the other shore. (If you had the rope further to the front, the canoe would start edging into shore; rope tied further back, the canoe would start edging out, until you would be pulling the canoe entirely sideways and hoping that the rope is not going to break, that you can hang on with no future relief, and that the river is kind to your canoe after you let go.) You are walking at a constant speed relative to the water. Now suppose you walk faster or the current increases. You are hoping that the increased force towards shore will be exactly counter balanced by the force of the water pushing the front end out. Experienced canoers find that in most cases the water wins, and here the canoe starts to push out, increasing the amount you have to pull, in a losing sequence.

Short ropes are useless as 1) the canoe needs to stay in deep water and 2) in water only just deep enough to float the canoe, there is a kind of suction at work that pulls back on the canoe–It seem like water in front of the canoe rushes back to fill the space where the canoe has been.

Another maxim is to always have the lighter end lead–Did you ever try to steer a canoe with the big guy in front? The front in this situation seems to have a mind of its own. With my canoe, after I got out of the canoe, the front end was the heavy end; at first I moved the green bag to the back to lighten the front end, but eventually came to reverse the canoe.

Jumping to the evolutionary cordeling prize, use a 50 foot, floating rope (not nylon), and tie one end as near as possible to the heavy end of the canoe (now called the stern) and the other end of the rope to about 5 to 7 feet back from the light end (now called the bow), near the seat. Twist the middle of the rope once around the middle of a 2 foot long, 1 to 2 inch diameter beaver-chewed stick, grab the stick with the rope between your fingers and start walking. Slide the stick up or down the rope until you find the sweet spot. Be ready with your other hand to pull more on the stern if the canoe starts coming to shore in calmer water or a wind shift towards shore or to pull more on the bow rope if the current picks up or the wind pushes away from shore, and then adjust the stick accordingly. In calm water stops have to be short because once the bow points towards shore, you usually can't turn it out by pulling on the stern. In current you can often rest and even take a picture (see slow picture on back cover). With other factors being the same your walking speed and the current determine where on the rope you should pull, i.e. hold the stick. If the canoe is approaching a rock, shallows, a calm spot, or an irrigation pipe you can adjust the stick a few inches towards the stern which will push the canoe out. The canoe will come to equilibrium again further from shore but with more resistance to your pulling; i.e. the further the canoe is from shore the harder the pull. But with a foot of water at say 10 feet off shore, the drag is small, even in current.

I am sure I am not the first to figure this out, but I never saw instructions or descriptions until this year in Sam Keith's book on Dick Proenneke: One Man's Wilderness, An Alaskan Odyssey. Like so many other things, Dick had it figured out.

#254 Cordeling in slow water, quick picture, red rope

#255 Irrigation setup ahead

On this day I was occasionally the center of attention as I sailed and paddled early in the morning. And when the wind died, I could cordel on a cowpath at the river's edge and a friendly sloping river bottom, at least to begin with. I loved it! It was like backpacking without a pack, seeing things along the shore I couldn't have seen from the canoe.

#256 Center of their attention

#257 Probably a bull snake; note water walkers

When I encountered 7 foot high banks with crevices to jump, it became a little tricky. When I had just jumped the third crevice (when does a crevice become a crevasse?) leaving my left hand trail as otherwise the canoe would not have let me jump, I snuck a look at the canoe and saw it had found a stiffer current and was veering out and pulling me with it. I quickly jumped backwards, grabbed the rope to the front further up which increased the pull momentarily, but allowed the back end to swing out and instantly relieve the pull; if I had missed my backwards jump, I would have lost the canoe to the river besides possibly hurting myself in the fall. Usually with the low water in the summer of 2005, there was room along the shore either on the shore or in shallow water. Now add rattlesnakes.

A wind came up strong against me towards evening. I waded up the river about 200 yards against the waves to the opening of Horsehead Creek and set up camp off to the side. I hiked to a low bluff and observed that the river is less than 200 yards wide when united, though often there were shallow forks with current. Made

Punjabi Choley (only a name to me) along with cous cous and pudding, cocoa drink, and Kool-Aid; had enough for lunch the next day. 10 miles

#258 View from bluff of river ahead, on CD only

#259 Horsehead Creek, on CD only

#260 Horsehead Creek, closeup, on CD only

Friday, July 15. Up by 7 a.m. with a placid river. I heard a noise I recognized but hadn't heard for a long time; it was a four-wheeler with the landowner, extremely friendly, who had come to investigate why his cows were looking this way all morning. He told me the story behind the name of the creek; as I remember there was a spring ice-dam break-up that caught a bunch of horses. I neglected to get his name, or if I did, I forgot to write it down. Using the Internet, I couldn't confirm the origin of the name Horsehead Creek, but the name existed in 1825 when another ice dam break killed 300 Sioux in the same area. Bummer.

#261 Friendly Landowner

174

#262 Probably another bull snake, on CD only

#263 Probably another piping plover nest, on CD only

Mild wind was against me all day. I spent half the time paddling, half cordeling. Camped at the Hazelton boat landing at about 7 p.m. and talked to Merit, the young park maintenance guy with his motorcycle. I climbed a nearby bluff. I noted that the former higher shoreline was not as obvious, implying that I was getting close to the former high water mark of Lake Oahe. 13 miles

#264 Islands in the sunset, on CD only

Saturday, July 16. Canoed from 8 to 8. Had good sailing at first but then the wind turned fickle and I was up and down with the sail and had to paddle/poddle. No good shore for cordeling. Lunched on last of bread and peanut butter, than again at McClain Bottoms on jerky, nuts and dried apples. Talked with Jerome and Mal, who were sighting in a 45/70 rifle for moose hunting in northern North Dakota in October, a very limited season apparently.

A gentle tail wind came up as I passed by a broad sandy beach area near Bismarck, called the "Desert", allowing me a 50 foot view of people and activities, mystifying a few weekenders as to my means of propulsion, as the wind was really slight. People had cars, beast trucks, 4 wheelers, volleyball games.

#265 Good times on the river

I camped a little further up on the west shore in the Oahe Wildlife Management Area, though, without my atlas, I didn't know it. I met Mel and his 2 kids from nearby Mandan, also camping. 15 miles

Sunday, July 17. Up at 7 with breakfast being a combination of oatmeal. polenta, grits, nuts, brown sugar, water and dried milk. Drank the last of the 5 gallons of water from Fort Yates, 3.5 days ago. I was ready to canoe into Bismarck, but after a mile I rounded a corner into a fierce and terminal northwest wind. I was in a forested river bottom with no chance of cordeling.

#266 Windbound again

Tied up the canoe on the east/north side and hiked along a dirt road in a general upriver direction. Got rides both ways for about half of the round trip distance of 14 miles to WalMart. Bought hot dogs for lunch, a North Dakota atlas, 10 pounds of dog food, 5 pounds of sugar, cookies, chocolate, fly swatter, 8 mm tent pole kit, and then a Montana Atlas at Scheels, thinking positive. Heavy load on way back. Picked up a gallon of water at Meredith's house, only 2 miles from camp. 1 mile

#267 Should have brought my backpack

Monday, July 18. Got going at 8 a.m. against a northwest wind that was only A (angry, not PO), and paddled the 6 miles to Abraham Lincoln State Park on the west (town of Mandan) side of the river across from Bismarck by 3 p.m. Toured On-a-Slant Village and learned that the Mandan and Hidatsu men procured the hefty cottonwood logs required for the lodges, but that the women built and owned them, housing large numbers of people, 30 to 50. I could see how the sod insulation could keep them warm in the winter. The state park people actually found native women who remembered how to make lodges and apparently supervised the building of the one pictured. These were the people near whom Lewis and Clark over-wintered, bartering for food. Also where Charbonneau was hired along with his 16 year old Shoshone wife, Sakakawea, which is North Dakotan for Sacajawea.

#268 Geese near shore

#269 Lodge at On-a-Slant Village

Sixty years after Lewis and Clark, when the fort was a going concern, a certain George Custer and his wife lived in the commander's house which has been well maintained. I toured that also in the company of a couple other tourists and young summer workers playing the parts of Custer, some military subordinates, and house cooks. The whole exhibit was well done and showed good effort on the part of the state–Hey, this is North Dakota after all.

During the time on the water, I saw bald eagles and flying families of geese with some molting happening apparently as I saw one adult lose 6 feathers at once. I also saw a family of mink momentarily outside of their den in a sandbank; kicked myself for not being quicker with the camera.

I enjoyed the campground facilities, shaved, showered, and loaded up with water. 6 miles

Tuesday, July 19. Canoed north 10 hours, 9 a.m. to 7 p.m. I was able to sail for a while early with a south wind until it blew too hard for sail. By 10 a.m. the wind had shifted to the northwest and strong from the west for the rest of the day. Near evening I got a Coke from Dora and Laurie Alfstad. After I set up camp below the Double Ditch Village site and put out a nightcrawler, they beached their pontoon boat and we had a nice chat. While we were talking, I caught a 19 inch catfish which I had for supper, with bread and cocoa.

Towards dark I climbed the 50 foot bluff to view the site and found a wonderful pair of Columbia brand leather sandals which I still use. 12 miles

#270 Sailing under the BN&SF bridge, same line as in Wisconsin

#271 View from Double Ditch Village

Wednesday, July 20. Up at 7 a.m. Took a better tour of the meadow above and saw about 100 depressions from teepee use, but gave a lousy picture. Radio-predicted south wind was a no-show; paddled against a weak northwest wind all day. Caught a sturgeon during lunch break. Met James Sheldon cayaking down from Three Forks, Montana. He had started on the west coast and used trucks to cross the mountains. I camped on a sand bar on the east side of the river across from the Square Buttes, named by Lewis and Clark. Supper was a 14 inch walleye, sourdough pancakes and pudding. 12 miles

#272 My first sturgeon on the trip

#273 James Sheldon

Thursday, July 21. Woke up to a good south wind but decided to climb on the west side. I think I ended up on Horseshoe Butte.

#274 Horseshoe Butte, on CD only

#275 View downstream, on CD only

#276 View of Square Buttes

#277 View upstream

Back on the river by noon, the wind was variable in both direction and strength. Couldn't cordel because I was back in real river bottom with too many shoreline trees; I had to paddle hard occasionally as the trees in the water pushed me out into the current just like a parked barge.

#278 Log-lined shore below Washburn

#279 Canoe on sand bar at lunch break, on CD only

I camped in the Washburn city park right on the river but with poor access. Met Kerry Beckman at the local cafe. While I talked with him and others, people and kids were feeding and petting Daisy. Kerry gave me a tour of the town in his truck. He works for the McClusky Water Project which takes water out of the east end of Lake Sakakawea, called Lake Audubon, and canals it for at least 70 miles, close to the headwaters of the Sheyenne River, which, amazingly, runs east all the way to the Red River and thus Hudson Bay. Not to be confused with the previously mentioned Cheyenne River which arises in the Black Hills of South Dakota and flows east and north into Lake Oahe and the Missouri.

INTERNET ASIDE: I looked up the McClusky Canal and found a strange story–the canal was built years ago along with a dam that created Lake Audubon 13 feet higher than Lake Sakakawea, with water pumps to lift the water to the higher lake. The canal holds water still due to millions of dollars of maintenance work each year, but it is basicly a dead end because North Dakota, Minnesota, Canada, and the U.S. Congress can't agree on money, route, and the goodness of Mo water mingling with Red River water. They do let some water out of the eastern portion to keep the canal water from stagnating but apparently aren't even irrigating where they could. Watch the news for more but don't hold your breath. I also found that the North Country Trail which runs from New York into North Dakota, ends after it follows the McClusky canal to Lake Audubon.

By 10 p.m. I had settled in for the night in the park when one of 2 camping lady bicyclists brought Daisy back to my tent, saying in polite terms, that the dog was a begging pest. I apologized and, not having a leash or rope near the tent, brought Daisy inside. She quickly barfed onto the tent floor and the lower part of my sleeping bag; I think it was the ice cream. It took 3 trips in the dark through the brush to the river for water to clean up the

tent and get a leash. All because the dog didn't STAY! where she belonged. Geez. 17 miles.

Friday, July 22. Took a picture of Al Thompson, a biker on the Lewis and Clark Trail from St. Louis to the Pacific Ocean. He was coincidently biking with the two lady bikers about whom I never did learn much.

#280 Al Thompson

I emptied my backpack and trekked a quarter mile to Main Street, found a laundromat and paid 75 cents for soap, $1.25 to wash, and 75 cents to dry my sticky clothes. Then hiked up the hill past the school to the grocery store and got $36 worth of bread, milk, orange juice, Kool-Aid, cocoa drink, breakfast rolls, 20 pounds of dog food, and bananas. Stopped at the laundromat and piled on the clothes on the way back to the park. Then I hiked about a mile west to the highways to tour the Lewis and Clark Interpretive Center for $7.50 My notes say I like it but I can't remember a thing about it now. When I was a kid touring the nation with my family, I thought museums were a waste of time. I enjoy them now (for an hour), but their lessons don't stick with me like my experiences exploring a river.

I left the park at about noon and stopped at the replica of Lewis and Clark's Fort Mandan about 3 miles upstream. Had a south wind which faded by evening but I remember making a wake as I sailed to a stop to chat with 5 friendly people on shore taking a rest from canoeing downstream but fighting the wind . Passed by a large fiberglass touring canoe painted to look like birchbark. Camped on the north side in view of a power station. Caught a 13 inch walleye. 9 miles

#282 Fort Mandan reconstruction

#283 Happy canoers

#284 Two canoes

Saturday, July 23. Caught a 30 inch sturgeon, a 5 pound carp, and an 18 inch walleye. Ate the 2 walleye and 3 eggs for breakfast. Left at noon. Fishing during the day in a narrow, deep sided channel, I had a northern about 2 feet long hit and get off of a Rapala, my closest encounter with a northern on the Missouri.

#285 Pretty fish, on CD only

#286 Adult eagles (left) take good care of their young

Had a west wind all day and I was going west or northwest, so cordeled, paddled, and poddled. The river level was down by 2 feet from the day before, maybe even lower later as the 6 to 8 p.m. paddling was pretty easy along the high west bank. I camped on a sand bar in view of the power generator of the Garrison Dam backing up Lake Sakakawea, 6 miles away. Ate pretzels, Kool-Aid, peanut butter and bread, milk from the gallon jug. 11 catfish, 5 walleyes so far. 13 miles

Sunday, July 24. Got an early start with a quick peanut butter and bread breakfast. River a foot lower still, little current along the edges.

#287 Picture break at 9:21 a.m.

#288 Cordeling in clear water, on CD only

#289 Easy shore for cordeling, note my foot prints,
canoe trail in water, on CD only

Nice sandy shore allowed easy cordeling the clear water. As I was loading up for the first carry, I noticed one of my tires was too low and that my new air pump was worthless. Curt and brother Neal offered to take me to Pick City for air; I had briefly met Curt, a pharmacist, back near Bismarck at McClain Bottoms where he and his wife were catching catfish. Today, he and Neal had caught 8 catfish (there is no legal limit). I bought a 12 pack of Pepsi at the gas station that gave me the free air.

#290 Garrison Dam holding back Lake Sakakawea

#291 Neal and Curt (right)

I wheeled the canoe without problem, though slow and hot. I had forgotten to add the backpack and one pail to the canoe, so had to carry these on the second wheeling. Keith the head ranger, waived my entry fee, offered to carry all my stuff in his truck, and eventually did give me a ride late in the evening to get water and pick up my charging cell phone at the park entrance. I hadn't forgotten the cell phone this time, I knew I would have to go back for water. Honest.

At the boat launch, a couple of fisherman gave me 3 small walleyes. I talked to a couple of other sailors as I sailed out of the marina. I canoed about a mile to just outside the park and had walleye (Yum), Kool-Aid (standard good), and generic Mac and Cheese (less than Yum). 9 miles

Monday, July 25. A north wind came up at night, flattened the tent at about 7 a.m., and was still blowing hard at 7:30 with rain until 11 a.m. I carried my cooking gear to a shelter in the park and made pudding and phone calls and remet Paul, one of the sailors from last night. Left about noon trying to go northwest with a north wind for about 5 miles. I took a great hike up an Observation Post with a good view upstream to the west. Back in the canoe, I was going west with a fading northwest wind, paddling with the sail up trying to tack into the wind. Must have worked some as I made 18 miles by 8 p.m.

#292 Next point of view

#293 Where I am going

Tuesday, July 26. Paddled from 8 a.m. to 11 a.m. until a west wind made me quit. I napped, lunched, fished, and hiked until 5 p.m. The lake was obviously lower than it had been years ago; the brush and grass had taken over but the washed rocks remain. Some of the rocks were long and round, suggesting petrified trees, but the idea of concretions offers an alternative explanation—the idea that rocks can form by directional natural forces, like stalagmites in a cave with dripping water. (More on concretions later.)

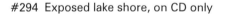

#294 Exposed lake shore, on CD only

#295 Probably concretions, not tree trunks

I had one strike on a diving blue Rapala, probably a small bass, and experimented on how hard it would be to catch one of the many ten pound carp cruising through the clear, greenish water. It wasn't hard at all, then I caught another when I was trying for catfish. I began throwing the carp onto the shore for scavengers. As I left this dry paradise, I paddled against a mild west wind, with more engaging scenery. I like this place.

#296 Large rock jumble

#297 Scenery right next door, on CD only

#298 Pretty valley an hour further uplake, on CD only

#299 Sentinel outpost another half hour further, on CD only

Camped on a bay close to Indian Hills Marina, though I don't know why my notes say that, as there is no name for the nearby boat access and campground in the Atlas. There must have been a sign on the lake shore proper, or perhaps I had another map. 12 miles

Wednesday, July 27. I paddled hard from 8 to 2, making 10 miles, turned a corner to go north and picked up a south wind that sailed me another 23 miles. I went by Independence Point and with my Atlas and GPS handy, turned west right after that, choosing to avoid the huge northern dead end of Lake

Sakakawea called the Van Hook Arm. I was able to continue sailing west with the south wind, but kept seeing attractions I wanted to explore. So I pulled in to camp around 6 p.m.

#300 American Point

#302 Inviting valley, unexplored, on CD only

#303 Camp, note flag on mast indicating wind direction

#304 Inviting valley, explored

As anticipated, I had a pleasant hike to the north. When I got to the top of the first hill, the 3 clam shells I saw amazed me--The spot was way above even the former high lake level; I can only think that a raccoon carried them there when the lake was high years ago.

#305 Go figure

There was an even higher view from the top of the box canyon to the north, so that's where I went.

#306 Next observation post

#307 Bay with camp, where I came from beyond, on CD only

#308 Upstream, i.e. uplake view, on CD only

#309 Another downstream look, too special not to include

As in all such hikes, I was gathering firewood on the way back when I picked up a 13 inch piece of stone which I had thought would be burnable. In spite of the theory of concretions, I'll continue to believe it is petrified wood until I learn differently.

#310 Unburnable prize pictured later in Wisconsin snow

A black dog ate my 3 leftover fry breads. To make these I incubate a yeast dough for a day in my aluminum pot with a plate for a cover (after I lost the original cover) in the only safe, available spot in the canoe–underneath the rear seat, and then fry a pancake-sized piece in a little oil. See Appendix 2 for recipe and procedure. I had the last of the store bread for lunch today, wondering what I'd have for lunch tomorrow–dog food? 24 miles

Thursday, July 28. The river turned to the north and like yesterday morning I paddled against a mild wind for about 18 miles to New Town and 4 Bears Casino in the Fort Berthold Res. Saw a coyote along the way there, close up in the rocks, but I was too slow with the camera. Cows and horses were more my speed.

#311 Highway 23 bridge near Newtown, ND

#312 Daisy herding livestock; actually cows often threatened her

Solved my lunch dilemma with an $8 buffet ($2 senior citizen discount) at the casino and made sure I got my green veggies. I met Troy Baker there, helping to survey the lake bottom in speed boats, one of which almost ran me over, so intent were they on their machines. Also talked to a young man, possibly Indian, who was interested in my trip but had no Internet connection for follow-up. I tried fishing twice in the afternoon with no luck. Passed through some high hills in the morning but the area for the 10 miles after the casino was as boring as the previous day was exciting. I was seeing geese families, pelicans without young, cormorants, gulls, but very few ducks. 23 miles GPS

Friday, July 29. Really windy from the east early morning. I was going west, so I tried but quit after about a half mile, just too crazy with big breaking waves; sailing was out of the question. The lake had a long straight section running nearly straight east to west, giving rise to big waves. I took 2 boring hikes in the flat former lake bed and then, with perhaps a little less wind, managed to get away from shore and do a fast drift without sail down wind. I found that the biggest (5 foot) waves would come in sets of 3 to 5 about every 20 waves, so I could relax a little between sets and move the canoe a little south to avoid the shore straight ahead. But the big ones would curl and white cap frequently; I had to make certain to keep the canoe parallel to the big waves, so that they didn't break into the boat–nerve-racking business, but I had already hiked the countryside, twice. I was sponging the boat between the big sets of waves. The wind eventually calmed enough that I could sail.

As I removed stuff from the canoe at camp that evening, I found two 3 inch minnows that had washed into the boat. The lake was all muddy and shallow (2 to 3 feet deep 30 feet out) near camp, but I tried fishing anyway and found that there was a feeding frenzy going on! I had a bite within a minute every time I threw in a nightcrawler, one of the 2 minnows, or a fish part on the bottom. I caught 7 catfish and a drum.

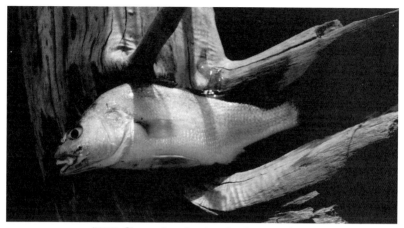

#313 Sheepshead, a.k.a. freshwater drum

Had 5 catfish and the drum for supper, all good, though in Wisconsin drum are considered a rough fish–helps to be hungry I suppose. It is hard to imagine the number of fish that must have been in that muddy water that they would find a worm always within a minute. I don't think that is enough time to find a worm by smell in that roiling water and there were drum there also, a fish that doesn't use smell as far as I know. With a 20 foot long seine, I doubt 2 men could lift the catch. I wonder if the Indians knew about this? But then they didn't have long straight reservoirs. 16 miles

INTERNET INFO: Family Sciaenidae, Genus Aplodinotas, Species grunniens, the freshwater sheepshead is the only member of the drum family not in salt water. With an adapted swim bladder it can produce a sound during the May and June spawning season. Its eggs float and are fertilized at the surface. It also has oversized ear bones (otoliths) up to an inch in diameter, which allow one to estimate fish age, up to 72 years in Red Lakes, Minnesota, 32 years in the Cahaba River of Alabama. Consensus of fishermen comments on the Internet is that the meat above the ribs is as good as walleye if fresh, skinned, and iced and the meat doesn't touch other fish parts. I think I heard the males drumming as I floated down the Big Sioux River about June 9; the canoe may have amplified the low moan. The sound would come and go, presumably because I was floating past and over them.

Saturday, July 30. Was able to sail with a mild east wind. I had been seeing great blue herons occasionally and finally got a reasonable picture of 3 birds today.

#314 Presumably 2 adults with a young one

The wind pooped out right after I found a well inflated plastic air mattress in the middle of the lake. I guess I knew that I was off the main channel but figured I would be all right following other current; I was wrong. The current spread out as I went upstream (in the middle of the lake!) and as I muddled, poddled and paddled through the mud towards some other current about 50 feet away, I became mud-bound. I got out to pull and sank up my mid-thighs. I crawled to the front of the canoe and managed to pull the canoe towards the current a few inches. A dark image formed briefly in my brain of late evening rain, lightening, wind, and misery. Returning to the possibilities here at midday, an idea slowly emerged involving the air mattress and a sprint to shore leaving the canoe until next year's rainfall–but no, Daisy and I both wouldn't fit on the mattress. Try again–the mattress and a rope, yeah. I lay on the mattress and doggie paddled to the side of the canoe where the cordeling rope was. As I wrestled with canoe innards, I slipped off the mattress and a west wind came up to blow it 20 feet away and gaining. I did the Sakakawea crawl about 50 feet before I caught up to it, not wanting to lose anything that floated out here in this vegetation-free swamp. I had to rest after I got back to the canoe, which of course hadn't budged. I tied the rope to the front of the canoe, paddled with the other end of the rope while lying on the mattress over to the current, buried myself up to my armpits in the mud, and pulled the canoe over to the current. I washed myself as best I could, crawled into the canoe and kick-washed my legs as I dragged the rest of me in without tipping the canoe. Thankfully, this current didn't disappear and I eventually got over to the main channel to the north and stayed with it. I went right by the Lewis and Clark State Park without recognizing it, probably because of the low water.

Instead I met Donna B and begged 3 gallons of water from her. She was enjoying the 102 degree (Internet says 101) weather at the shore but took me back to her home (in a development of homes) in her golf cart, giving me and the water a ride back to the canoe also.

#315 Thank you, Donna B

A favorable wind came up that allowed me to sail another 5 miles past mud shores. I camped at the only possibility, a narrow strip of dry land, nearly covered with willows. Got there by struggling through mud up to my knees; I walked the shore a quarter mile to find water surrounded by firm mud to wash myself. I see now on the Atlas that this strip of land was County Road 42 before the Garrison Dam, now re-emerging. There were hordes of mosquitoes by nightfall. I hoped that we were away from tickland and let Daisy in (I had washed her also), really worried for her. I decorated the inside of the tent with the 50 mosquitoes that came in with her before I could sleep. 16 miles

Sunday, July 31. Hard day, wind my way but mild, paddled all day, sometimes with sail. Current mild but relentless. HOT as yesterday (Internet says only 95). I couldn't cordel as couldn't walk in mud or in the willows (thick as grass) where there was real land. I took a hike around 11 a.m.

#316 Upriver view, canoe near shore

#317 View of old driftwood, stuck in valley years ago, on CD only

#318 Area to the north, on CD only

I had been seeing ducks, pelicans, gulls, terns, but no eagles. Had a great wind for the last 2 miles, sailing right up the river's best current instead of poking around the edges. Camped on a nice big sand bar with only a few mosquitoes during daylight and wind; they came out in force by dark. As I was close to Williston, I used cell phone to call kids, change my home message, and call Bob B. to report latest set of GPS points to put on my sistersfarm.com web site. 12 miles

#319 Wide river, showing cliffs south of Williston, on CD only

Monday, August 1. Since I am always in the tent by dark at about 9 with at most an hour looking at maps, writing journal or eating, I had little problem awaking early, though I claim I didn't sleep well the whole trip. By the way, the camera goes through AA batteries at a pretty good clip, but I can reuse them in my mini flashlight and the cook stove fan for days of use.

Today I was up at 6:30 and did my journal for the last 3 days, eventful enough that I could still remember them pretty well. Then I cooked a breakfast. I planned to go WalMarting as I wanted to clear my photos in anticipation of some scenic river and land in Montana. I never saw an early access to Williston so canoed to the far north side of the Highway 85 bridge. I emptied my backpack, gathered 5 empty gallon milk jugs, and started the 5 mile hike to WalMart. I left the jugs at 4848th street on the right about a half mile away. Soon after that a young man in a van, Jim, gave Daisy and me a ride right to WalMart. He had just been to Medora in the North Dakota badlands on the Little Missouri; I had considered heading that way if I were running out of time for Montana, so I was interested in what he had to say about the area. I think "dry" was the shortened summary. I still don't know how far one might canoe into that river from its junction with the Missouri, but it looks to be perhaps the wildest section of the plains.

I checked my cell phone at the door like an honest phone slinger and picked up my usual supplies and lunch treat. I made

CD's also but instead of clearing my memory card, I bought another 1 gigabyte card for $85; I still have almost all my photos on these cards as I bought 2 more when I returned home for only $30 each.

As I was putting a leash on my babe magnet, Nancy and Kathy from Canada began to talk with me about my trip.

#320 Nancy and Kathy, I forgot the order

They had been at a high school reunion in their home town in Saskatchewan and had come to Williston for shopping. Before I could talk long enough to let them know what a mean, rotten, and dangerous person I was, Daisy convinced them to give us a ride back to the river where I took their picture. Much as I hated to separate, I thanked them profusely and had them drop me off near my water jugs. I begged water from Belva Leer who quickly and graciously accommodated me, but wouldn't let me go that easily.

#322 Belva Leer

She called her husband Wade, knowing that he would be interested in my trip. Wade interrupted his carpentry job to come visit and give me a ride to the canoe with the 5 gallons of water. I believe he is now a school teacher doing carpentry during the summer, but he was telling me about organizing and running a community water supply at one time. I had hoped he would write a story for my first book, but he probably couldn't find the time.

OK! What great people, eh? Canadians and their near relatives in North Dakota, eh. I got the canoe ready to shove off and mentally started a check list to see if I had done everything I wanted to in Williston and somehow the location of the cell phone came up–still charging back at WalMart! "Those women, those flustering, good looking, trim Canadians!" he said with the smile of a horny fool. About the time I should have been picking up the cell phone at the Service Center, I was trying my best to be a cool, tough, worldly, but sensitive mountain man.

Not wanting to start a 10 mile hike at 5 p.m., I did what any shamed mountain man would do, begged a ride off of Wade. After he dropped me off I still had time to sail about 2 miles up the river. 7 miles

Tuesday, August 2. The wind was a little help today at times, but lots of paddling in heat. River very curvy of course; I was heading southwest on average. I roped and paddled, as the shore and bottom were too soft for poddling. Camped on a sand bar with Ronrick Thomas who was on a kayak trip from Billings, Montana, to perhaps Key West.

#323 Apparently oil here besides mud, on CD only

#324 Ronrick Thomas

He was low on supplies so I gave him 2 quarts of dried veggies and about 8 buffalo chips, hamburger-sized jerky. We had pudding together. Mosquitoes really bad after dark. I forgot to take a GPS reading here on this day but it happened to be the only camp site I hit twice, second time in November. 11 miles

Wednesday, August 3. About dawn an absurd west wind came up and blew the edges of the tent up, pulling the wire stakes out of the sand, losing 2 or 3 of them. It wouldn't have been a problem except for the mosquitoes last night–I had peed in a cup and didn't want to open the netting even to throw it out. I threw the tent and sleeping bag into Mo to wash off the urine, knowing I'd be sleeping in both for another few months. The wind was only A as I paddled, poddled, and cordeled against it in the rain, reaching the confluence with the Yellowstone and the Confluence Interpretive Center about 3 p.m.

#325 The Confluence, the Yellowstone entering from the left

#326 An historic site, on CD only

The $5 entry fee included dry heat in the center and a tour of the restored Fort Buford the next day; camping was free. I hung things to dry in a shelter near the boat dock and toured the Center. Rain stopped at 3 and the sun came out to dry my stuff at about 6. I tried fishing at the dock without luck. Wendy and her relatives at their family reunion treated me as one of the family with hot dogs, chips, cold pop, and rice crispy candy at camp. 5 miles

#327 Wendy and daughter, how nice!

Thursday, August 4. I was awoken by a crop duster who seemed to be making circles over my tent. For breakfast I had 3 hot dogs with buns from Wendy's crew. I met Diane at Fort Buford for a personal tour of the Officer house with Lewis and Clark information and then of the newly restored barracks for about 60 men with kitchen.

#328 Diane in the barracks

I then visited the cemetery, mailed the CD from Williston and some North Dakota info to Polly and bought 3 Lewis and Clark momentos, 2 specially wrapped candy bars and a metal cup.

#329 Rough life out here

#330 Ditto, on CD only

I paddled about a half mile past the Highway 58 bridge and cut into the woods north to visit Fort Union, afraid that it was out of sight from the river; wrong and a bad idea with rampant river bottom growth. I should have gone another mile and would have seen the fort, though still miserable access through mud. Passing between maintenance buildings, I met Ranger Randy Carr who showed me a better path back and pointed towards the fort. I spent a nice time in the fort except that I forgot a leash for Daisy, they had not even 2 feet of rope, and she was being a pain, I think even chasing a rabbit around for a while. Richard, role-playing the trader was entertaining and educational, knowing furs, fur preparation, trapping, and the goods they were traded for. I think he was the one who told me that the real traders would trade with the Indian kids for mouse skins, mostly for good will, but used them for glove liners. I believe Richard lives close to the land even when not in the fort.

#331 The river never rests

#332 Fort Union from the river

I hiked back to the maintenance area where Randy gave me a short ride and then walked with me to the river in sight of the canoe; he mentioned a welcome-to-Montana sign on the west side of the fort. So after I had paddled up to the fort area, I hiked through knee-deep mud past the fort and to the sign and got a picture of the fort from the west, showing how it looks with Indian tepees.

#333 Made it to Montana!

#334 Fort Union as it might have looked in 1830, on CD only

I then paddled a half mile past an old Railroad lift bridge that was used by wagons and autos until 1985 and camped. Why a lift bridge on Mo? Because Fort Benson, many miles upriver, was at one time the busiest port in the USA. Well, for tall steam boats. Well, it was busy. Honest. 6 miles First camp in Montana!

#412 Snowden lift bridge, still used by BN&SF, but not lifted

INTERNET STEAMBOAT REALITY CHECK: The steamboat era through here to Fort Benton (below the Great Falls) only lasted 27 years with the peak of 50 boats in the season of 1867. This time spanned the Montana gold rush that started in 1860 and the desire for goods in northwest USA and in southwest Canada. The railroad to Helena pretty much put them out of the freight hauling business in 1887. But 50 boats a year probably didn't compete with St. Louis, probably not even St. Paul.

Chapter 11

Montana Mo

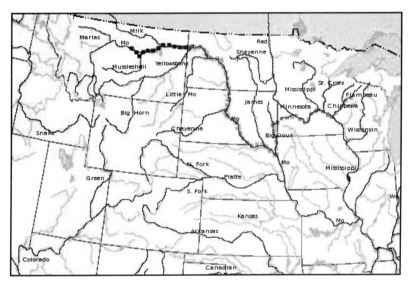

#413 Canoeing the Missouri River in eastern Montana

Friday, August 5.   Tough day, mild wind with me in the morning, upwind after that, but current not too strong. Saw one shore riprapped with old tires. A lot of sand bars, some mud. Wonderful river views. River curvy as usual. At camp I fished with grasshoppers and caught 2 goldeye shad. These goldeye act like trout in watching the surface. I cut strips of meat off the back of one, fished on the bottom and caught a big chub (In Wisconsin people eat chubs out of the Great Lakes, but only smoked.) and a small catfish I threw back. Made couscous with my dried veggies plus pudding for supper. 8 miles

#414 , on CD only

#415 Old tires protecting shore, on CD only

#416

#417 Goldeye (top) and chub

#418 Break to climb

#419 Downriver view

#420 Camp and beyond; canoe is dot next to log, on CD only

#421 North view, on CD only

#423 Islands ahead

#424 Cabin in the sagebrush, on CD only

#425 First Montana gully

214

#426

Saturday, August 6. Wind against me in the morning so hiked to the north up a Missouri break (#418). Found Montana to be North Dakota on steroids. No phone service in camp and phone about dead anyway. Nice canoeing against a gentle current and little wind, good views from the river also. Canoed to the Highway 16 bridge by 6 p.m. Treated to hot dogs, bratwurst, 2 hamburgers by 3 Sioux, 1 Assiniboine, 1 Pomo/Sioux plus kids. Walked 3 miles into Culbertson, charged the cell phone, bought $17 of snacks and supplies, called kids, Capital One, brother Jon and changed the 30 second message on my home phone. Walked back in dark, in bed by 10:30. I forgot to get water, have 3 gallons to get to Poplar. 96 degrees at 7:30 p.m., store people said a high of 106. 11 miles

#428 Generous grillers; Keenan in background

#429 Road to Culbertson, on CD only

INTERNET REALITY CHECK: Wolf Point only
registered a high of 95, but the high the next day was 102.

Sunday, August 7.   Up by 6:30, breakfast of a little chicken,
hot dogs, old pancakes. Mosquitoes bad until a little wind came
up behind me but the wind was never enough to sail with and
then turned against me besides, medium strength. Current easier
than the Mississippi, the Minnesota, or lower Missouri, but
shallow near the shore so had to stay out often in deeper
somewhat faster water because of suction effect mentioned
before.

Keenan from Culbertson caught up with me just to talk; he
had seen me briefly the evening before at the bridge and boat
launch. He has spent a lifetime in the area, lots of different jobs
but currently calls himself a ditch-digger, married to a Native
American. I wanted him and his wife to write for me in my first
book but too busy I guess.

I was tired from my long day and hike into town yesterday and
stopped by 6 p.m. But the area was too inviting.

#431 BN&SF again

216

#432 Keenan

#433 Bluff near camp, on CD only

I hiked to the north ridge for a view of the river and what lay away from the river. A wheat farmer and his son were probably tired by the end of the day also, certainly dirty and sweaty, but still curious enough to drive over in their pickup to see how a figure came to appear on their horizon towards the river. "Canoeing" says I. "Where'd you put in?" says he. "Wisconsin" says I. "You're shitting me!" says he. But I think I made their day; I know he made my day and made it into my book. 7 miles

#434 Next observation post

#435 View of tomorrow's river

#436 Harvesting wheat

Monday, August 8. Canoed 8:30 to 8. Had good wind at times, especially once when I sailed right up the main current for about 2 miles. Stopped at Brockton after about 12 miles and bought $20 of cookies, Kool-Aid, Raman noodles, half gallon of milk, small orange juice, 4 large butterfingers and begged some water. At camp, I guess I thought I should document the area, so took a picture of the bluff across the river that ordinarily I would ignore. Could hardly believe my eyes 30 minutes later, though you have to use the CD and see the difference in color. 14 miles

#438 Don't like this picture? See next picture, on CD only

#439 Thirty minutes later, on CD only

Tuesday, August 9. Hard day, paddling against a mild wind and usual river current. Passed under an unnamed highway bridge with Sprole to the north. Scenery was ho-hum at best. Aldo Leopold wrote about how a pound of grouse can liven up a ho-hum forest; a different bird livened up this shore for me.

#440 Young red tailed hawk

Maybe I should clarify what I mean by a "hard day". Mostly it means that, because of wind, faster current, or poor bank conditions for cordeling, I didn't make as many miles as I would have in better conditions and of course got tired earlier in the day. Or it could refer to rain, sleet, snow, or cold, hardly ever to heat unless I couldn't find shade. A "hard day" certainly doesn't mean that I was wishing I was elsewhere doing something easier; I was having a ball. My body was tuned and ready to paddle, push, drag, walk, or whatever, taking each day as river recreation and as somewhat of a challenge. On a "hard day", I might have to quit canoeing early and hike, fish, or nap, or I might continue anyway, depending on my options. I knew that any difficulties or discomfort I had, including the mud, would be temporary. Especially now that I had actually made it to Montana, I had even less reason to push myself and I intended to take full advantage of what I expected to be better scenery, fishing, and hiking. Still, if I wanted to keep seeing new things, I had to paddle faster than the current. 9 miles

Wednesday, August 10. Thunderstorm and about a third inch of rain last night. Had mild wind with me then against me as I paddled to the dump near Poplar. The friendly cook-out people at the Culbertson bridge and Keenan had mentioned Ed and his Busy Bee Cybercafe as an Internet access point. Sure enough Ed helped me email Polly one of my border crossing pictures and I caught up on my email for something like 10 bucks I think, good deal whatever it was. Ed used to be in a rock band (possibly with Keenan) but now considers rock music the devil's own. I think he was born again after witnessing a (possibly drug induced) revelation/miracle involving a bright light if I remember correctly. Anyhow, he seemed to be doing good things for the town and people around Poplar and certainly was good to me.

I did some grocery shopping and hiked the half mile back to the canoe, realized I had left my journal at the cafe, caught a ride there, hiked back to the canoe again to find my tackle box missing. I had talked to a kid fishing near the canoe upon my first return but then saw 3 kids leaving the area as I returned the second time. As I canoed upstream, I came upon the 3 fishing along with the BIG older brother of the original fisherkid. I explained my trip and the situation to all until big brother said "Austin, give him back his tackle box." Austin claimed he didn't know where it was, but fisherkid got it for me. I didn't realize until later that Austin had already taken some things out of the box plus things out of the canoe including sinkers, clippers, old knife, and hemostat. I was especially disappointed in the missing sharpening stone, Gerber saw, and night crawlers as they might impact my trip directly and soon. I assume their dog ate my loaf of bread and Austin ate the orange. I worry for you, Austin.

I camped on the other side of the river in view of Poplar. A thunderstorm with a quarter inch of rain came up around midnight; the wind bent the tent poles but didn't break any. Sirens sounded and it looked like a fire in downtown Poplar. 4 miles

Thursday, August 11. Stiff wind against me most of the day. Had the last of my bread with peanut butter for breakfast. Just as the hawk made my day 2 days ago, I think I made the "thing of the day" for some cows. I could still see Poplar water tower at my first break. Stopped at a whirlpool and fished with grasshoppers on bottom with no luck. I took another hike at camp, but the observation posts were lower and further. The views were pleasant, but exciting only to a farmer. 4 miles

#442

#443 A poorly placed observation post, on CD only

#444 View back, on CD only

#445 View ahead, on CD only

Friday, August 12. Less wind than yesterday, but still against me from the northwest until river curved to the south and I could sail to the Highway 13 bridge, where I took a break. I met Wayne as he was returning from Wolf Point on his 16 inch bike with 20 pounds of meat for his dogs salvaged from a dumpster. He gave me 4 pounds for Daisy. He lives in a camper inside of a barn and has to carry his water in from town. Hard, cold day; I wore a long sleeve shirt for the first time since Minnesota. I camped on an island in view of his barn. 13 miles

#446 Wayne, nice guy

Saturday, August 13. (4 months of trip!) Weather was cold the night before, but warmed up nicely this day. The water was colder and clearer. Had eggs, oatmeal, polenta, and hot cocoa for breakfast. Crossed over the channel and talked to Wayne for a while. He generously gave me 3 gallons of water, knowing that I would have to carry it a distance if I got it in Wolf Point. (He fires up his truck occasionally to get his water.) He used to take care of the farm for a trio of disparate owners and still does to a lesser extent. He told me that one spring one owner planted something, maybe sorghum, and midsummer one of the other owners, not recognizing sorghum, "disked them ugly weeds right down."

Left about 10 a.m. Paddled to an apparent road entrance to Wolf Point and local fishing spot. Met Kyle Reddog, wife Dianne and 3 kids fishing. They may have watched canoe for me as I walked the half mile into town. I had been thinking about how to let my friends know (i.e. how to brag appropriately) that I had made it to Montana if and when that happened. I also had been

222

wanting to see some of my better pictures from my new camera on paper and came up with the idea of a personal post card rather than a standard Montana souvenir picture of a cowboy on a horse; this is why I crossed the mud into Montana at the border. Ed had suggested the Wolf Point Radio Shack. I got there on a Friday, but a quick survey of people in Wolf Point indicated a good liklihood that it was really a Saturday, and, sure enough, the post card lady was not working. Her kind co-workers suggested Hi Tech Photo Studios, called up the owner, and brought me over to his studio. Dennis Brockmeyer agreed to give up lawn mowing, met me there and efficiently made me 100 post cards for just $50, but not until he had taken me back to the canoe to get an adapter for the camera that I should have brought. Cool! Dennis wrote a short story for my first book; he was also a deputy sheriff, a detective, a deputy coroner, and still was a deputy state livestock inspector. I bought a $70 fishing license, $26 of groceries (where Dennis found me to return my recharged cell phone) and then paddled a couple more miles. 5 miles

#448 Hello Wisconsin!

#449 Pretty horses

#450 Restful oak prairie

Sunday, August 14. Hard day, stiff wind against me until evening when I was too tired to do more. Fished midday but only caught 3 goldeye, kept one. The huge Fort Peck Indian Reservation borders the river on the north; I didn't learn much about it but enjoyed seeing their horses and an oak prairie. Apparently W. Clark had passed by in 1805 and left his name in a recently excavated sand bank; I thought this was cute enough to include here, especially since they got the year right–The real signing along the Yellowstone was done in 1806 and Lewis and

Clark really did pass through here in 1805. I enclose 2 pictures of an irrigation pump. Note how the current increases as I move out to pass the pipe. At evening fishing I used a goldeye strip and, in the presence of lots of mosquito witnesses, caught a 17 inch sauger, a close relative of the walleye and of the perch that doesn't get as big as can a walleye. I tied the fishing pole to the canoe and left bait out overnight. 7 miles

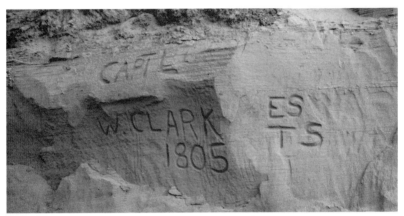

#451 Bill was here (?)

#452 Irrigation pump

#453 Have to paddle hard to get around, on cd only

Monday, August 15. I had a 19 inch catfish on the line in the morning (note spots on the dorsal fin of sauger that distinguish them from walleye), so cooked fish for breakfast and had some leftover (16 fish meals already for only $170!). Moderate wind against me all day, even after the river made a U-turn! Saw an old skull I thought might be a buffalo head, but was reminded later that buffalo horns go up, not forward. Daisy cleared the 50 geese off an island for camp. Tried fishing but only got a small sauger that I threw back. Scenery didn't encourage a hike. Supper was 1 cup minute rice, 1 cup dried veggies, 2 cups water, half a catfish filet, with soy sauce. Darkness about 8:15 p.m. MDT. 9 miles

#454 Catfish, sauger, goldeye

#455 Cow head, on CD only

Tuesday, August 16. I was usually going west with an east wind but the river had 3 oxbows so I had to paddle several times. But mostly I sailed for 12 hours until a storm from the west snuffed out the east wind.

#457 on CD only

#458 The geese and I, flying downwind, upstream

From camp I hiked up a hill on the south side of Mo and saw where I came from, the Milk River coming in from Canada and Glacier Park, and my first view of Lake Fort Peck. Saw 10 mule deer, 1 cottontail rabbit and 1 jack rabbit on hike; Daisy chased after all of them. 14 miles

#459 Radio Tower Hill, on CD only

#460 Downriver, on CD only

#461 Milk River, top water

#462 First view of Lake Fort Peck

Wednesday, August 17. I met Ron Garwood on his land on the north side of the river; Ron wrote a great story about his family history and Montana life for my first book.

Sometime during the last few days, I encountered two wide rapids with inhospitable shores that I had to wade up in about knee deep water, towing the canoe. This day I paddled through an area called the Dredge Cuts where a lot of fill had been extracted for the Fort Peck dam and then I camped in the park about a mile from the power houses.

While touring the Fort Peck Interpretive Center, I met Ron Bondy. I traded a meal at the Missouri Outpost for use of his clothes washer, and we tried fishing at the center with no luck, though we did see a dead 30 inch lake trout. 6 miles

#464 Fort Peck Dam, power house

#465 Ron Bondy

Thursday, August 18. Enough wind last night that I slept without the tent but with a mosquito head net. Less than ideal with a little rain, but OK. I took a better look at the center, toured the power house, showered, shaved, wrote post cards. The history of the building of the dam in the depression era and what it meant to Montana residents both as employment with good wages and as a displacing force was well told in their displays and movies.

Then I left my camping stuff and wheeled the canoe about 5 miles over the dam to the Fort Peck Marina, a homey, family run operation. I met 14 year old Amy, mother Terra, and Grandma. On the way I found and used the Post Office, buying 70 stamps and of course talking with the postmistress. After Amy showed me the slip where I could leave my canoe, I returned to the Marina office to find a care package in my canoe of 10 monster chocolate chip cookies from the postmistress's daughter, along with a nice note. Brought the canoe the short distance to the slip and then hiked back to camp.

I slept in the open again, but poorly. Sometime during the groggy night, I was interviewed by police as some one had stolen a black box of GPS equipment; as my black box was furry, they let me go. 0 miles

Friday, August 19. Up at 7, finished writing 12 post cards and mailed them on the way to the Marina with my ice chest and camping gear. Bought a breakfast of Snickers, Fritos, and Dr. Pepper at the Marina. Amy filled my water jugs and brought them to the dock with her 4 wheeled Mule.

#466 Amy with Mule

I updated the home phone message and talked with Polly, then left the Marina about 9:30 a.m. Had a strong north or northwest wind as I was going south on Fort Peck Lake. I talked to some fisherpeople on the lake and found that there was a lady's fishing tournament starting the next day; I can't remember whether it was for walleye or bass or maybe even catfish. Sailed and paddled both, but then had to stop when lake turned a little more west or perhaps the wind shifted to the south with high waves coming at me. It seems that the winds are more likely to be either with me or against me rather than across the lake; I think the surrounding hills channel the wind. I camped at what the map calls Fifth Ridge from the dam, though with the low water, the actual number could have been higher. It was also The Pines Recreation Area, with a good road all the way down the ridge to the point, though no one else was there. I took a rest on a concrete picnic table with a good view. I took a hike and saw 3 mule and 1 whitetail doe deer. Nice sunset. 16 miles

#467 View of sky at 90 degrees, on CD only

#468 Sunset, on CD only

Saturday, August 20. Up at 7:30, mild wind in my favor, allowing for good sailing, only needed to paddle occasionally. I didn't know that loons flock up in the fall.

#469 Rare as a flock of loons

#470 Full sail

I don't think I have explained my sail setup entirely. It is called a lateen 45 square foot sail, made by Grumman for their standard canoes; my canoe was nonstandard, a Grumman Eagle, and I had to modify the rudder attachment. The discoloration is from Daisy blood when she jumped in the canoe after a fight and before I could stop to wash the sail. The patch on the upper right was sewn on for me by Eileen Ziesler before I left home. The 3 smaller red patches are fabric tape I put on to stabilize small rips. Without wind the sail is collapsed with the hinge on the lower left and detached from the mast (but with the ropes still attached), and lays along the inside of the canoe where dogs can bleed on it. When a wind comes up, it only takes a minute to pull on the hoisting rope (seen at lower left over the green bag) until the sail fills out some, then with my right hand insert the boom slot into the mast, put a foot on the boom sheet while hoisting the top of the sail frame (I'll bet that has a name also! Wait, it does, I just found it–the gaff spar.) to near the top of the mast, then wrap the hoisting sheet onto a cleat near the rear seat, grab the boom sheet and let it out appropriately (looks like a tail wind here) while steering with either hand on the square rudder handle behind me. I don't understand why the hoisting rope in the picture looks slack over the green bag; it runs through an unseen pulley at the bottom of the mast and is usually taut to hold up the sail. Perhaps it is tangled in front of the yellow map case or maybe it actually is taut.

The sequence for lowering the sail would be to turn the canoe so the boom can be grasped, unwrap the hoisting sheet from its cleat, and let the sail fall into the canoe. I had leeboards also shown in early pictures; since I couldn't reach them to raise or lower them, I sent them home with Kevin in South Dakota.

Almost missed my turn off into Hell Creek Bay, Marina, and State Park at about 7 p.m. The lake was so low that tying up was a mystery including that there didn't seem to be access to the park. Clint helped me find a slip on their dock at the Marina. I bought a $5.50 2 piece chicken supper with bones and skin for

Daisy. I found their water OK with ice but extremely bad the next day at 90 degrees. 19 miles

Sunday, August 21. I wrote more postcards for a total of 56 and sent them with Debbie to mail on her trip to Jordan; she added 10 zip codes for me there before mailing them. I bought grapefruit juice and bread and packed my butt pack for a day's hike in the badlands of the west. Though I didn't know exactly what a "break" was or what the Missouri Breaks looked like, people seemed to agree that the area across the bay was pretty similar.

The area starting about 6 miles to the west included Hell Creek and the digs where Jack Horn found the Tyrannosaurus Rex exhibited at the Center, Fort Peck's Rex. So I was looking for dinosaur bones also, but knowing that, between my ignorance and bone scarcity, finding any would be improbable.

I had a great hike with fascinating non-Wisconsin scenery. I saw 7 mule deer does through the day. I took about 60 pictures and include here a good sample, sidestepping any impossibly useful description of these amazing badlands.

#472 Area of hike, across the bay

#473 Hinterlands from first ridge

#474 View to north of bay and lake

#475 As green as it gets, on CD only

#476 One of 4 vultures circling me

#477 Other side of canyon, on CD only

#478 Getting dryer, on CD only

#479 Pinnacle I aimed for, I think, on CD only

#480 First mushroom cap, harder rock shielding softer

#481

#482 on CD only

#484 Rocky

#485 Higher canyon, on CD only

#486, on CD only

#488

#489

#491 Yucca

#492 Prickly pear cactus

#493 Juniper

#494 Pines

#495 Sage brush

#497 Oasis, stagnant water

#498 on CD only

#499

I saw a high point in the near distance and went for it, recording its position, later finding it as a pinnacle on my atlas (elevation 2866 feet) 4.3 miles southeast of the marina (elevation 2010 feet).

I took several pictures of the arid vegetation: yucca, possibly Yucca glauca, in the Lily family along with onions, asparagus, and Aloe vera); prickly pear; juniper; ponderosa pine; sage brush. I started to circle back to the southwest at the pinnacle (there are other pinnacles on the map also, but none nearby). I continued to find entertaining scenery.

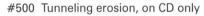

#500 Tunneling erosion, on CD only

#501 Ghouls

#502 Looking back at pinnacle from the west, on CD only

#503 North towards the lake, on CD only

#504 on CD only

#505 Power posts, no lines, on CD only

#506 Unexpected

#507 on CD only

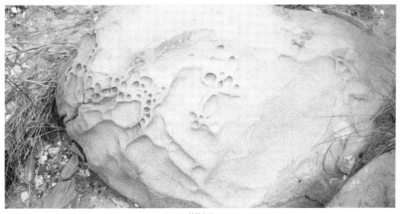

#508

#509 Salty surface of intermittent creek; self portrait, on CD only

I found no dinosaur bones but in gullys below drop-offs, I did find 3 spherical concretions, supposedly made by precipitation or binding of carbonates of various types; the dark color of these particular ones is possibly due to the presence of iron carbonate, or perhaps manganese carbonate. How a spherical concretion is formed and why they come out exactly the same size doesn't seem to be well explained. I have my own theory for this which I'll explain with evidence later in the book.

#510 Spherical concretions

Debbie said 102 degrees for a high. (Internet said only 94, but that was in Glasgow, 45 miles north.) I hiked from about 10 a.m. to 7 p.m., about 4 miles too long for optimum enjoyment– i.e. my ass was dragging on the return, as I cut too far south and had to follow Ried Coulee back to the south end of the bay, and then to the canoe. After the hike I treated myself and Daisy to the 4 piece chicken dinner. 0 miles GPS

Monday, August 22. Up at 6:45, wrote 7 more cards. I charged some supplies onto a credit card and got $40 cash besides, an act of trust and generosity on their part. I paddled out of Hell Creek Bay and caught the East Wind Express the rest of the day except the last half hour. If I had not just hiked the day before, I would have jumped out here (#512).

#512 Beauty snubbed

#513

I did stop at the Bone Trail Boat Launch, hoping the boating activity there was due to dinosaur bone diggers and that I could help dig, but it was due to hunting and fishing outfitters and their clients. As I paddled to turn around and leave, I broke the 42 year old white ash paddle my dad had made for me when I bought my first canoe; the lesson of becoming just too damn old was not lost on me. My other paddle that I had made for the trip was still sturdy, still heavy and considerably younger.

I tried fishing from camp without luck. The wind died completely. I heard an elk bugle in the evening and a coyote howl that night within 50 yards. 25 miles

Tuesday, August 23. I paddled 7 and a half hours past pretty land and then took a 2 hour hike to the west in the U L Bend Wilderness, saw 2 mule deer, elk tracks, and elk scat, but no dinosaur bone or digs.

#514 Pretty land passed by

#515 Hiking area, on CD only

#516 One observation post I didn't climb

#517

All of Fort Peck Lake is contained in the Charles M. Russell National Wildlife Refuge which extends up the river another 20 miles upstream of the lake also. Russell was a self-taught artist in the early 20th century who specialized in plains images.

#519 The Scout by C. M. Russell

I couldn't find out who Mr. Bend was, though it is quite a coincidence that there is this long bending oxbow that borders the U L Bend National Wildlife Refuge that contains the Wilderness, all of which is surrounded by the bigger CMRNWR. (The best guess of Beverly Skinner of the UL Bend NWR was that there was a cattle ranch with a brand of UL in the area.)

After my hike, I canoed another 4 hours, tied up to a snag and caught 8 catfish 13 to 15 inches in a half hour, keeping 6 of them. I camped nearby as wind from the northwest increased. As I was cooking fish, a gust came up and blew the whole works into the dirt: windshield, stove, fry pan, and fish; I think Daisy got most of that pan of fish. No rain until 2 a.m. when I put up the tent. 15 miles

#520 Great blue heron heading for the hills

#521 Lake Fort Peck "forest"; in upper lake, on CD only

Wednesday, August 24. UL Bend bottoms out about 12 miles south of the otherwise pretty straight east/west course of the lake. I paddled for just 2 miles until I turned the corner to the south and met the full force of the wind. Having good options, I took a wonderful 6 hour hike to the west, around Brandon Butte–neat rock formations, 19 bighorn sheep, 5 mule deer and a big cedar tree growing on a rock. 2 miles

#522 Next observation post

#523

#524

#525 Mushroom Cap with a capital C, downriver view

#527 An appreciation of roots

#528 Herd of sheep, on CD only

#529 on CD only

#530 The lake ahead, on CD only

248

Thursday, August 25. Saw a 10 point buck (western 5x5) from the tent in the early morning, too dark for a picture. Stiff wind against me as I left the lake behind me and paddled southwest into mud flats left by a higher lake. Took a 3.5 hour hike to west, seeing about 30 antelope, 8 mule deer, 10 sharp tail grouse, 1 cottontail. Hiked through a large burned area.

#531 View downriver, on CD only

#532 Mule deer antler

#533 Broken elk antler

Paddled another 2 miles through the mud and mild current or in main current without mud, also hard, wind against me still. To get to shore and camp, I sat on the bow and pushed with my feet as I paddled for about 200 yards–part of the legacy of the Army Corps of Engineers. 7 miles

534 Big sky sunset, on CD only

Friday, August 26. Another tough day against wind, current, and mud; I didn't see any alternative to continuing the push–the only thing that might have changed was the wind, and it could have gotten worse. Current through mud on the left and on the right. To get back in the channel from camp or to get started after a break or muddy mistake, I had to push the canoe on my hands and knees; standing I sank to my knees. My notes remind me that one time I needed a distraction and mental lift enough that I leaned over the side of the canoe on my knees in the mud and drank a warm Wild Cherry Pepsi. I did get a good picture of these charming shore birds, western willets I am pretty sure.

#536 Mud left

#537 Mud right, on CD only

#538 Willets

#539 Willets in flight, on CD only

The river depth did get better around 4 p.m. Found a close bank to the south around 7 p.m. and took it for camp. Caught 19 and 21 inch catfish, threw back a 6 inch chub and 12 inch catfish. I set out to hike but had to do a small circle as I was on an island at the bottom of the bend. The Musselshell River of central Montana enters from the south here, but I couldn't see any current. 5 miles

#541 Cracked mud

#542 Lots of cracked mud, on CD only

Saturday, August 27. I cooked the catfish in the big pan, 2 batches, including scraps and rear half of backbones for Daisy. Only have a half ration of dog food left after today. She'll get Mac and Cheese, buffalo jerky, fried fish, and other people food. Missouri River water is muddy from the wind and current but

251

clears up nicely with 12 hours of settling in a milk jug. I use it when boiling anything and it tastes good, possibly from herbicides, pesticides, or simply cow shit. The shore bottom was firm enough here to poddle off the island. After a short paddle, I took a 3 hour hike to the west and circled back. The first picture (#543) looks back at the bottom of the UL Bend as the river flows east. Third picture (#545) shows an old road through the sage brush and the fourth picture a view from the plateau with the Little Rocky Mountains about 40 miles to the northwest. Saw some elk sign, only 1 rabbit,1 grouse, but got good pictures of a hawk as I thought at the time, but matches up best with the bird book pictures of osprey.

#543 Skinny river behind

#544 Pines for a long way, east I think, on CD only

#545 Who, what, when and why?

#546 View northwest

#547 Big raptor

#548 Out of focus, but pattern of an osprey, on CD only

As I continued paddling, I saw pelicans as usual and a deer just before camp. At night I heard lots of coyote howls and elk bugles from 4 different directions. 6 miles

Sunday, August 28. Hard day paddling against current and slight west wind as going northwest. Poddled off of the bank for 2 miles. Took a short hike during the day for another look at the Little Rocky Mountains, which I had never heard of. For supper I split the Mac and Cheese with dog; she got 2 buffalo chips also, I got a cup of dried veggies. Late evening hike just up the hill behind camp, I heard a bugle across the river; the light was so weak and weird that I could see the reflection of the 4x4

253

bull in the water better than the bull itself–my first elk view. Lots of night hawks; they seemed smaller than those in Wisconsin, a size difference confirmed by at least one bird book. 8 miles

#550 Little Rockies, magnified, on CD only

#551 Sunset upriver, on CD only

Monday, August 29. Cooked 1.5 cups dry oatmeal with 3 cups river water and split with Daisy. Filtering half a gallon of settled water took at least 10 minutes of hard pushing, no fun. Started canoeing about 10 a.m. and was able to cordel from a cowpath until noon and then a mild tail wind arose to help me paddle until about 5 when it increased to sailing power and I sailed until 6:30. Saw an elk cow and then got a good picture of a calf as I sailed silently by. First sightings of magpies and I was seeing cottonwood trees again. Good day. I was out of the mud, even camped in sagebrush. I could hear a wind rising about 10 p.m. 15 miles

#552

#553 One of very few signs of past habitation

#554 Wary but young

#555 At camp, looking downstream

Tuesday, August 30. Besides half the oatmeal, Daisy got jerky and fish bones; I got oatmeal with brown sugar and nuts and 1 small catfish. Going west on average and had a stiff west wind all day, so took a 2 hour hike to the north. Saw 1 grouse. Another good day (mud free!) roping and paddling. Camped with John Deyo from Great Falls at the Rock Creek boat launch. He and several other hunters were scouting for the Saturday bow and arrow elk hunt; apparently the bull elk grow some hefty racks here. John gave me 3 pint bottles of water and a bunch of small wieners that Daisy and I shared. 5 miles, but included 2 oxbows

#556 Elk habitat, downriver

#557 Ditto, upriver, on CD only

Wednesday, August 31. Hard west wind against me so cordeled all but 1 mile. Lots of beaver sign. Spied a garter snake eyeing a leopard frog. Saw about 10 elk coming out of the willows to drink. Rested at Slippery Ann campsite on edge of a No Hunting viewing area. Continued on to Highway 191 Fred Robinson Bridge where I camped with Nate Stevane and Craig Krzycki at the James Kipp Recreation Area. They had seen me cordeling from a bluff on the south side as they were scouting. They grilled me 3 wonderful elk steaks with cheese and gave me

7 pounds of frozen elk and antelope steak and hamburger to carry with me; Daisy was treated that night also. They were trying to make room for this year's possible elk. I had picked up a small Styrofoam cooler as litter that worked out perfectly. I paid $6 for camping, but took 8 gallons of water with me the next day, a great trade as I was out of water. 9 miles

#559 Beaver channel, on CD only

#560 Elk along right shore, on CD only

#561 Snake and frog

Thursday, September 1. I was going to get an early start canoeing until I talked to the campground host, Al, who offered to shop for me when he went to Lewiston to fetch a trailer of water. I gave him $20 and he got me 20 pounds of dog food, 5 pounds of sugar, 20 packs of Kool-Aid, 2 loaves of bread and other things; I think he undercharged me.

#562 Al Dvorak

#563 Ross Eply (left) and Eric Oldenburg

While waiting for Al to return I met Eric and Ross of Bozeman, Montana. Eric's graduate student project at Montana State was to study and help the endangered pallid sturgeon and they were dumping tagged foot long young fish into the river. There were reading stations up and down the river to monitor their movement and existence. They shared their lunch with me (including fresh carrots from Eric's grandmother's garden) and offered to help me portage from Mo headwaters into the Yellowstone later in the trip, near Bozeman.

Another interesting but seasonal event here and on other parts of the Missouri and the Yellowstone Rivers is the paddlefish snagging season, in late April. Especially at the first diversion dam on the Yellowstone River above Lake Sakakawea, the Yellowstone Caviar Program prepares snagged female paddlefish (Montana record 142 pounds) for fishermen in exchange for their eggs, i.e. caviar. They share 30% of the profits with the Montana Fish, Wildlife, and Parks Department, which the FWP uses for paddlefish research. The Caviar Program distributes their share of the profits by way of grants to Eastern Montana entities. I also saw buildings and informational signs related to caviar on the Missouri here and back at the Confluence; I assume these are extensions of the Yellowstone Caviar Program, but couldn't verify that on the Internet. The paddlefish snagged in the Missouri of Montana come out of Fort Peck Lake and are limited to 500 per year, perhaps 4% of the population. Both populations are doing well apparently, but require constant monitoring.

Some interesting information on paddlefish and their caviar from an article by Andrew McKean in Montana Outdoors includes that females only spawn every third year but may contain about 5 pounds of eggs, the caviar sold retail for $300 per pound in 2007, other sources are being depleted, and that, compared to trout fishing, "Paddlefishing is more like dragging a river for sunken logs."

I also met Steve Miller of Merrill, Wisconsin, there to hunt also. Steve gave me a pound of sausage and some smoked Great Lakes salmon, both very good and especially useful in that they would keep while I was eating the thawing meat.

At mid-afternoon after Al returned, I canoed under the Highway 191 bridge into the official Missouri Breaks. 3 miles

#564 Missouri Breaks ahead

Chapter 12

The Missouri Breaks

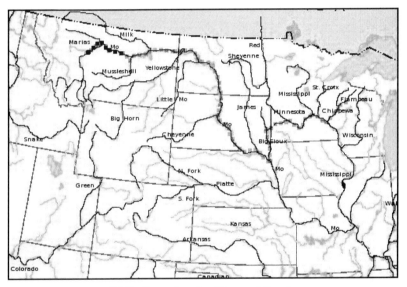

#565 Canoeing the Missouri Breaks

Friday, September 2. I cooked elk steak for breakfast with lots
leftover for lunch. Cordeled about two thirds of the time,
paddled the rest with a little poddling off the bottom, but the
bottom is gravelly now and the paddle slips often. Current varies,
sometimes easy. Area starting to look too dry for elk, but saw 3
elk, 2 mulies, lots of cows, and beaver sign. Passed by some old
farming sites. I couldn't find the first campground, aptly named
Hideway Recreation Area, and camped about 2 miles downriver
of the Lower Woodhawk site. Cooked a veggie stew with steak
and hamburger; Daisy got a half pound of hamburger. 11 miles

261

#566 Now familiar scenery, cordeling; still love it, on CD only

#567

#568 Scenery, on CD only

#569 Mule deer below cow, on CD only

#570 Beaver access

#571

Saturday, September 3. Bow and arrow elk season starts today. Comparing different hunting seasons, archery is the best way to see the natural world. In the gun season one has to wear blaze orange, hardly camouflaging, to avoid getting shot; for most other hunting one doesn't have to be especially stealthy to get game. However turkey hunting is restricted to shotguns, and with the well-known wariness of these birds, one has to be well camouflaged and sneaky to get within range or to call them into range. To give hunters more advantage, spring turkey seasons and archery seasons usually contain the rutting season of the animal, when the males are occasionally pretty dumb, or at least less wary and often on the move.

Lower Woodhawk campground was not marked either, but I talked to 2 elk hunters and a girl friend there. I was cordeling when we met and one of the hunters cracked something to the effect of "not going very far that way." As I pointed out that, other than sailing with a strong tail wind, this is my fastest way of travel, I realized that I was really arguing against American tradition and for a better travel philosophy–that by going upstream, I was seeing the scenery 3 times longer than those going downstream, that recreational travel (and all travel if possible) should be enjoyable by itself, not as a daily leg of a race. There are those who think that any exertion while recreating should be avoided, but, as long as my body doesn't complain too loudly, I am not one of those.

I was roping and paddling equally during this day. Daisy was ahead of me as I was cordeling through grass along a faint animal trail when I noticed her nose swing to the left momentarily. Reasonable dogs like her don't bark at night without a cause, disobey only if they think they know better, and don't take an extra sniff unless there is extra smell. I looked to the left with maybe a half step in that direction and saw my first coiled rattlesnake! It wasn't rattling but obviously was unhappy that I found him or her and had already decided whether to go for my bare leg or right through my tennis shoe. I took a picture but the snake is barely visible in the grass. I decided to wear my hiking boots with high leather when cordeling, even though the water would probably ruin them. This, like all the rattlesnakes I saw, was a reasonable, well-behaved snake, certainly not aggressive. I was glad that Daisy didn't find reptile to be an enticing smell.

I passed by 2 campgrounds and Cow Creek coming in from the north (the unmarked crossing of the Nez Perce National Historic Trail). Began to see some big cottonwoods the beavers hadn't gotten to yet and appreciated them as a new source of

#573 Good cordeling, close to Cow Creek

shade. I think I have enough experience now to say that I was seeing classic Missouri breaks and standard badland erosion and loving it; living here would be something else, but an interesting thought if I could be near the river.

#574 Dry hills, nice shade, on CD only

#575 Classic Missouri Break

#576 Standard erosion for the area

I camped for the next 2 nights at an unnamed site near the old Gist farm on the north side. As I was setting up camp I heard a loud crack, like rock falling on rock. I looked around and, across the river, saw 2 full-curl rams peacefully grazing. I saw them often over the next 2 days and never saw them head-butt, but never heard that noise again either. 5 miles

#577 Bluff across river from camp

#578 Close up of rams near water, 45 minutes later, on CD only

Sunday, September 4. The entire river from Fort Benton to the James Kipp Recreation Area (149 river miles) is designated as the Upper Missouri National Wild and Scenic River; the Upper Missouri Breaks National Monument is also involved. Information in a BLM brochure mentions and my Atlas illustrates a lot of private land inside and around these boundaries. But, for a hike into the Breaks, there was a 225 square mile piece of BLM land that extended 15 miles north from where I was camped. As I was looking at the Atlas in camp, I noticed the Gilmore cabin about 4 miles straight north and figured that would be a worthy goal, though not important enough to figure out how to enter its coordinates into my GPS and then use the GPS as a pointer. I had breakfast, packed my butt pack with survival gear, water, and lunch, set out 2.5 gallons of river water in the sun, and headed past the Gist buildings and north.

#580 Old Gist farm and Little Bullwhacker Creek, on CD only

#581 Some farm buildings

#582 Rabbit, on CD only

#583 The road north

It turned out that there was a road that dead-ended at the rabbit-infested Gist farm and it came from the Gilmore cabin; I spent a wonderful couple of hours following this road which meandered along the valley of dry Little Bullwhacker Creek with some fantastic views. After the cut I climbed some more and got a view back, where I could barely see Mo and the Judith Mountains further south, maximum elevation 5600 feet about 50 miles away. There were more impressive views still before reaching the cabin. The cabin has been donated to the BLM by the Gilmore family, some of whom still visit occasionally. The BLM maintains the cabin and fences around it, and the cabin is open to anyone who wants to use it. It has a bedroom with bunk beds but no mattresses and a living room/kitchen without water but possibly with a wood stove, though I can't remember for sure.

#584 The road from above, on CD only

#585 Mushroom caps

#586 Broken fence, benches (narrow plateaus) beyond, on CD only

#587 on CD only

#588 The cut

#589 Looking back at the top of the cut

#590 Judith Mountains, looking south

#591 Taller mushrooms, on CD only

I read through most of the journal entries over the last 6 years. There was some good hunting 4 to 6 years ago for ram, buck, bull, and mountain lion, but nothing since then. Other than the Gist Farm rabbits, I was not destined to see any wildlife this day and very little scat. I assumed that the area was now too dry, though I can't explain how so many cows survive; perhaps because they don't spend the whole year here or because they have hidden water holes.

Regarding the ongoing debate in the journal between hikers, hunters and cow punchers, I put myself down as a tree-hugging hunter who could tolerate a reasonable number of cows. The cattle people wanted to claim that the area and cabin came into the public domain because of ranchers and cattle grazing which, to me, is true, self-serving, and irrelevant–without cattle the place would probably be supporting more wildlife and looking even better, and I can't imagine any other private enterprise using the land. I suppose there might not be the minimal access by 4-wheel drive vehicles that there is now, but river access would have continued. And I guess that the land could have fallen into private hands with "No Trespassing" signs on the boundaries. So I am glad that public ownership evolved and if running a reasonable number of cattle keeps the local ranchers in business and happy, so be it.

#592

#593 The Gilmore cabin

#594 Little Rockies, east, 5,600 feet, 25 miles

#595 Bears Paw Mountains, northwest, 6,900 feet, 40 miles, on CD only

After lunch at the cabin I took a half mile hike east to the end of a knife sharp ridge for some long distance views. Cool! I have canoed to the mountains!

Back to the cabin, I headed northwest along one of 2 roads heading away from the river and then cross country in the same direction. In picture #598, I saw my first short-needled evergreen (I assume to be a fir) to the left of the ponderosa pine in the picture. I observed a fence, more cattle, and a watering hole, probably the narrow spike of private land from the north that I see on the atlas that divides the 2 Bullwhacker Creeks, and I entered the Big Bullwhacker drainage system.

#597 Sage brush and pine, on CD only

#598 Fir or no, not doing well, on CD only

#599 Water

As I was trekking down a dry feeder coulee, I observed one of the oddest things I've probably ever seen, though at the time a row of clay bowling balls seemed a natural fit to this arid landscape. It was obvious to me that these balls had all started from the same place as mud falling from an overhang and had grown (like snowballs down a snow hill with packy snow) as they rolled down a muddy slope until they bumped into each other, though I didn't look for the assumed slope.

#600 Set up the pins!

Having picked up 3 identically sized spherical concretions in the Hell Creek area (admittedly 110 miles away, see picture #510), I naturally assumed that similar clay balls had landed in the concave basins of the gully where I found them and had been rolled around by the occasional water flow into a smaller uniformly sized compact sphere; it seems, however, that I may be the only one who believes that. (I should point out that there are small protuberances on two of the 3 concretions which shouldn't be there if friction was causing the roundness; perhaps spherical concretion formation involves both smoothing by friction and addition by precipitation–J.B. Kurz, very amateur geologist.)

The return trip down Big Bullwhacker seemed unnecessarily long and hot, but nonetheless interesting.

#601 View down Bowling Alley Coulee

#602 After junction, view down Big Bullwhacker Creek, on CD only

#603 Dry peak

#604 Same site further left

#605 Same site as #603, even further left, fellow shade seekers

I had the best shower of my life with my 2.5 gallons of sun-warmed water; Daisy hit the river. The skies were darkening but I heard just one thunder as the storm passed to the south. I made pudding and drank Kool-Aid as the wind switched from east to south.

#606 View back up Big Bullwhacker Creek from Gist farm, on CD only

Towards late evening I went down to the river to welcome James Clinton and several Indian students from the college in Poplar. As you might expect from the only black engineer in Montana, he was ready for anything, including my request to write a story for my first book; in fact he wrote a second story about Chief Joseph, so appropriate because we met only a few miles above Cow Creek, where Chief Joseph and what was left of his Nez Perce tribe had crossed the Missouri before surrendering in the Bears Paw Mountains.

#607 Students from Fort Peck Community College

The rams were still there and James got the best picture of them which we put in my first book. We shared a camp fire and some cooked fish they had caught, but sleep was pretty heavy in the air. 0 miles, but I'll be back

Monday, September 5, Labor Day. James saw me off early in the morning. I moved the canoe nearly entirely by cordeling which was almost like another hike except that I kept going over the tops of my boots in the water.

#609 View back towards Gist farm, on CD only
#610 Same site, view across river, on CD only

I saw 3 flocks of pigeons around the river cliffs, 15 to 30 in each flock. The next six pictures are what I saw cordeling between 9 and noon, including the color of a rattlesnake tongue:

#611 Typical riverside view, on CD only

#612 Good cordeling with good view

#613 Same site, right side

#614 Ditto, a little more left, on CD only

#615 Erosion at work, on CD only

#616 Purple!

I spent just 30 minutes from 2:30 to 3 p.m. investigating the mouth of a little unimposing coulee north of the river which nevertheless amazed this naive Wisconsin boy; I took the next six pictures there.

#618 Coulee entrance

#619 Brown and white, on CD only

#620 Same site, close up

#621 Same site, with river

#622 Upriver, on CD only

#623 Straight up

#624 Gotta see this

While cordeling, I found a garter snake very involved in eating a toad. Then at camp I had great luck fishing. I caught a 6 inch chub with my last bit of worm. I cut the chub into bait and caught a 14 and 25 inch catfish (my biggest), an 18 inch sauger and a 12 inch goldeye. I found that I didn't care much for my dried apples (too bad because I had 5 gallons of them), I think because they were too sweet. This day I boiled some in Mo water for some delicious apple juice. Great day. 11 miles

#625 Garter snake with hands

#627 Goldeye, small cat, sauger, big cat

Tuesday, September 6. I fried fish for breakfast; I came to like catfish as much as walleye. Unlike walleye however, one has to cook the catfish thoroughly or it stalls at rubber. I sliced the filets on the bigger catfish sideways, lengthwise to make them thinner and more easily cooked. I packed and started sailing with an east wind about 11 a.m., but between changing directions and just dying completely, it wasn't much help early. Somehow took in 15 gallons of river once. Saw herds of about 9 mule deer and 14 sheep with about 5 rams, biggest horns at about half curl. So paddled with sail most of day but was able to rest and just sail 3 times when I was going south or southeast.

#629 Mule deer, on CD only

#630 Sheep

Camped at the McClelland/Stafford Ferry and met Grace Sanford, the colorful, sweet, and less-than-young operator. She gave me fresh corn and potatoes which were great but too hot after cooking; as we left them to cool and shared my chocolate pudding in the house, her blind dog ate most of my supper. I am glad that Grace was able to write her story for our book before she died in 2007. Her daughter, Susan, runs the ferry now; Susan contributed the only (short) story close to poetry in our book. 8 miles

#631 McClelland Ferry

#632 View from north towards Winifred, on CD only

#633 Grace responding

#634 Grace at the helm, on CD only

Wednesday, September 7. Down to 1 gallon of water. Spent the day roping and hiking; took 2 days to dry the inside of my boots and now they are wet again. Saw a flock of about 10 Hungarian partridge from the canoe and took a picture of a magpie. Hiked north of the river for about 3 hours, found a cave, had a helluva good time.

#635 Daisy and magpie, on CD only

#636 Valley to explore, on CD only

#637 Hill with cave, on CD only

#638 Inside of cave

#639 View back down valley, on CD only

#640 View up, on CD only

#641 A struggling, perforated community

#642 Facial features close up

#643 View back towards river

#644 Coming down with Daisy

#645 Vertical erosion from up, can't go just anywhere here, on CD only

Back on the river I met 3 canoes going from Coal Banks Landing to James Kipp Recreation Area. Found a rapids which was easy cordeling but would have been an impossible paddle and a hard walk (See Picture #930 on back cover.). I was seeing Canada geese flying, nights and mornings, along with a few geese and ducks on the river. This day I saw a bald eagle and a small hawk with a robin-sized bird in its talons. 7 miles

#648 Reward for ascending rapids, the right to paddle slowly, on CD only

#649 Evening delight

Thursday, September 8. I have no idea what this McKenzie drift boat was doing here, but it is the best picture I have of them; it is the boat of choice on most Montana trout streams for a guide and one or two trout fishermen; this one has a square end for motor attachment.

#651 McKenzie drift boat

#652 PN bridge at Judith Landing, on CD only

I cordeled 5 miles to the Judith Landing and the PN bridge, named for the Powers & Norse ranch on the south side where Grace's son-in-law works. While cordeling I saw racoon tracks, saw and heard kingfishers, and now have seen 4 rattlesnakes, including 2 at one site–don't take your eyes off your next step around here and certainly don't jump just because you saw a snake. I had a nice break with Brenda and her beer drinking friend at her Trading Post; she couldn't part with any significant amount of water. I bought 2 Hershey bars, a Dr. Pepper, and a Klondike ice cream bar.

The river was deeper above the entrance of the Judith River and I paddled the rest of the day. This river was named by Clark for his future wife and runs north out of the Little Belt Mountains with a small contribution arising in the Judith Mountains. I camped at The Wall Recreation Area, an oasis of shade and evidently a rabbit refuge. I met Ron and Cindy from California and Lance and Dianne from Oregon; Ron filtered me 3 gallons of water overnight, using a large filter and about 5 feet of gravity; saved me a half of a day spent boiling water. I had sourdough pancakes for supper and boiled up some more apple juice. 10 miles

#653 Long distance views are often majestic, on CD only

#654 Camp in the cottonwoods

#655 Rabbit and signs of beaver with big teeth and bigger ideas

Friday, September 9. Before leaving, I took a picture of the flat prairie dog town above camp, perhaps not worth showing without any animals. I saw some the day before, bigger than I thought, between a gopher and a woodchuck. (I noticed on the Internet that the UL Bend area was a site for the blackfooted ferret recovery program, a weasel that lives only near prairie dog towns.) Daisy chased a rabbit through camp.

I roped for about 8 miles and paddled for 2 miles.

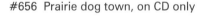

#656 Prairie dog town, on CD only

#658 Easy paddling

#659 Good trail but obstacles in the water

#660 Cordeling 20 minutes later; note reversed canoe

#661 Nice trail, but may run aground in the bay, on CD only

Wind was brisk to strong against me in the afternoon. Occasionally heard rooster pheasants and saw some different shore birds, probably the greater yellow-leg, took a few pictures of a great blue heron in flight.

#662 Same size as willet but color says it is a greater yellowlegs

#663 Great blue heron left of cow, on CD only

288

Thunder and rain while cooking fry bread in camp. Took a hike after supper and the rain. 10 miles

#664

#665 on CD only

#666

#667 on CD only

#668 My only portrait-oriented picture;
Daisy posing at bottom, on CD only

#669 River view from the rocks, on CD only

Saturday, September 10. Still a stiff wind against me and rainy, about 50 degrees, in the morning. Stayed that way with less rain the rest of the day. I cordeled and managed to keep the insides of my boots dry for a change, taking pictures occasionally.

#670 View of spires while cordeling, on CD only

#671 Pyramids with attitude, on CD only

#672 How many years to appear thusly?

Took a morning break at a campsite where the cottonwood trees were protected with chicken wire.

#673 Beaver-proofed, on CD only

Met and shared fry bread with Gary and daughter Erin. They gave me phone numbers of Great Falls Canoe Club volunteers who help people portage the Falls area. They have an arrangement for mileage reimbursement with the companies that own the dams that almost demand portaging. I have a photo of the numbers in the next chapter.

#674 Erin and Gary Fortenberry

#676 Jim and Daisy

The wind got worse and the river more shallow, broke rope twice trying to coax the canoe over shallows. Quit and took my last hike in the Breaks, into a northern valley that wasn't very impressive from the river (#677); nonetheless I took 47 pictures. The 6 pictures starting with #681 were taken basically at the same spot, within 5 minutes from the first to the last. Couldn't get away from this amazing scenery. The dark mound across the river in the picture #688 is probably Square Butte, a foothill to the Little Belt Mountains in the Lewis and Clark National Forest. I would be seeing these mountains during the rest of the month; the

Missouri makes a quarter circle as it flows north from Yellowstone Park and then curves to flow east. The line of dark rock marching up the left center of the same picture is a geological dyke, magma that was forced upward into a crack in the earth's surface that then resisted erosion more than the sedimentary sandstone around it. It is shown to better advantage in the next picture. As I climbed up, I took a picture of the site of the 6 pictures. I tried to circle back to the canoe, but had to search for an alternate route back down the steep bluff.

#677 Valley to explore

#678 Usual amazing view, on CD only

#679 Unusually resistant rock, on CD only

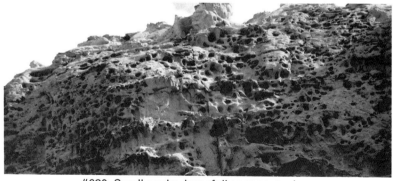

#680 Small pocks, hopefully not contagious

#681 Impressive drop, on CD only

#682 These protectors won't last forever

#683 River view, on CD only

#684 Larger view, on CD only

#685 Bare mound, on CD only

#686 Uphill view, on CD only

#687 View from even higher

#688 Dyke with flat butte in the distance, on CD only

#689 Better view of the dyke

#690 View of site of pictures #681 to #686; note bare mound, on CD only

#691 Aborted path down, on CD only

#692 Actual path down, on CD only

At camp, I tried to extend my buffalo-veggie soup with balls of rye flour paste (i.e. dumplings) which were at best OK. Tried fishing upstream about a mile with another hike but no luck. Saw 5 mulies at dusk including a 4x4 buck. 5 miles, great day!

#693 Camp, on CD only

#694 Late river view from camp, on CD only

Sunday, September 11. Cold morning, I'd guess 45 degrees. Made oatmeal per usual and cocoa drink. The background color of the scenery now includes some white, so I must be approaching the white cliffs. Had to rope again; though wind was less than yesterday, it was strong and persistent from the west. Found a large, light-colored rattlesnake and got a very close picture. My guide to reptiles suggests that the only rattlesnake in Montana is the prairie rattlesnake and that the postocular white line (behind the eye) passes behind the corner of the mouth. The next picture shows both white lines quite well but not the corner of the mouth.

#696 Nice introduction to the White Cliffs

#697 Needs no introduction, on CD only

#698 Probably a prairie rattler

I casted here and there as I cordeled, especially the deeper holes in front of coulees. Managed to go over my boot tops again. Threw back a small walleye on a crayfish imitation, kept a 13 inch smallie on a sonic and a 17 inch sauger on a Rapala. Ate them for supper along with the last cup of minute rice with soy sauce. Supporting backdrop hard to beat. 5 miles

#699 White cliffs from near camp, on CD only

Monday, September 12. Oatmeal breakfast, sourdough pancake with last of my maple syrup for lunch, fresh fry bread, Raman noodles with 1 cup of dried veggies and a buffalo chip for supper. Had frost in the morning. Three quarters roping, rest paddling, sandals in water about half the time or else watching my path carefully, avoiding grass. I've been seeing pheasants the last 4 days. Saw 2 mule deer today plus Daisy chased her second deer across the river–I could see a deer swimming with a small black head behind it; can't make her stop chasing deer. White Cliffs are impressive and I took several pictures but no hikes.

#700 Small castle, on CD only

#701 on CD only

#702 Vigorous sage brush, on CD only

#703 on CD only

#704 on CD only

#705 Picture from first book

#706 Pack rat, rousted by Daisy, above swallow nests, on CD only

#707 Back view, on CD only

Out of them by 3 p.m., had a meeting of similarly great minds at about 4:30, and then paddled until 5:30, camping close to Little Sandy Creek camp site, 5 miles to Coal Banks (the beginning of many down river trips) and about 40 miles to Fort Benton. Slower river allowed me to paddle after leaving the White Cliffs; mild west wind today. 10 miles

#708 In conference

Tuesday, September 13. 5 months out! Moderate southwest wind against me. Fished without luck. Saw about 5 mulies, pigeons, 5 pelicans, lots of geese, a few ducks, a second coot/mudhen. Took a few pictures but scenery no longer amazing, just entertaining.

I had a nice visit with the camp hosts at Coal Banks Landing, Shirley and Leon. They recommended a visit to the Virgelle Mercantile, a store off the river, which turned out to be about a 2 mile hot hike but very worthwhile, meeting Don Sorenson, buying rice, sugar, candy, peanut butter, 2 loaves of bread, ice cream and V8 juice for $14, his cost in Fort Benton but selling it out here in the sticks (hell, not even sticks out here), seeing his antiques, and receiving a free ride back to the canoe. Don's store partner Jim Griffin is the Virgelle Ferry operator and he wrote a wonderful story for my first book about finding his rainbow's end here near the Missouri Breaks. Canoeing was half roping, half paddling. 9 miles

Wednesday, September 14. Strong southwest wind against me all day so I was mostly roping. Saw 12 mule deer and my seventh rattlesnake, also a lighter colored, long, stout snake. Had my sandals on but being very careful.

#710 High bluffs, on CD only

#711 Don't tread on me! on CD only

Stepped into water to get back into canoe and found 4 feet not 4 inches depth, got all wet, including the camera; it really did seem to be water resistant, Pentax Optio33WR. In spite of cold mornings, the sunny days were still nice and warm and I dried out quickly. Took a short hike before camp and saw farm land to the south and the Little Belt Mountains to the southwest. I could hear my first traffic in a long time, from Loma. It was real tough cordeling, hopping the rocks that were stabilizing the old railroad that ran close to the river for miles on the north side, but between wind and current, I couldn't paddle; I think the south shore was too shallow for cordeling. Took my time. Tried fishing at camp but no go. 9 miles

#712 Farm land, on CD only

#713 Mountains

Thursday, September 15. I canoed up the Marias River about a half mile to within sight of the Highway 87 bridge. I hiked into Loma with cell phone and backpack stuffed with dirty clothes. I had a relaxing time in Loma, no groceries or laundromat, but good phone charging and service. I bought and ate snacks in between phone calls and charging. I used the phone to talk to Jim Adkins about portaging Great Falls. Stopped at 3 Rivers Canoe outfitters/casino/tavern and had an informative talk with Dale Hankins, a former county commissioner who thought they were taking good care of the Breaks before the Federal "interference". I wanted his story for my first book but didn't get it. Dale donated and installed a better antenna in my cell phone and gave me a CD of my latest 500 pictures which I sent to Polly. Back on the river, there were 12 to 15 jon boats with big Mercury outboard engines screwing around. I asked someone whether they were setting up for a race and he didn't want to say yes or no. I camped with this outfit at Wood Bottom Recreation Area. I was treated to snacks and then invited for supper and the next day's breakfast. Other people's food and cooking were very difficult to refuse. 2 miles

#714 Whose reality is this?

Friday, September 16. All the meals were catered and great. Had a nice chat with Terry, a Lewiston outfitter with his 2 high school boys, hired here as drivers I think. Entertaining talks with Rob Story, director of the jon boat race/fiasco. Everyone was sworn to secrecy, but I don't think I am violating any trust now, 2.5 years later and more by the time you read this. I think there was supposed to be some drama between the race drivers, probably about at the level of professional wrestling; most of the "racers" were Montana extras it seemed. There were some canoes involved today which was part of a "Reality TV" series called "Treasure Hunters".

But Rob Story had a good story, though I couldn't get him to write it down for my book. His grandfather or great grandfather homesteaded land along the upper Yellowstone near Emigrant, an hour upriver from Livingston. He invited me to launch my canoe there. The grandfather brought longhorn cattle to Montana (from Texas I think) and made several trips to Los Angeles by horseback for business. Rob left home himself for LA at something like 16 staking out black sheep status in the family without competition if I recall the story correctly. He stuck it out with his quick mind and stubbornness and has been working with TV and movies ever since, but lately at least, on his own terms. He is married and raising his kids on the old farm in Montana, taking care of his dad, and sharing the land with a brother who is a hunting guide. Spends a lot of time on "special" projects like this I guess. More later.

I remember paddling hard against current and wind as I left mid-morning, but the rest of the day was cordeling southwest until the last hour when I got to sail a little. The river seemed to have a lot of current and curves this day; evidence for curves are supported by the Atlas. 6 miles

#715 on CD only

#716, on CD only

#717

#718 The western flicker is red-shafted, not yellow, on CD only

Saturday, September 17. Rained a quarter inch overnight and sprinkled most of the day. Cordeled most of the day for 5 miles to Fort Benton and the end of the Scenic River status of the Missouri. Mo was swift and shallow here so paddling was out of the question.

I met Lefty from the UP of Michigan on the way into town as he came out of his travel trailer in the city park. As we walked together to downtown, he pointed out some historic and current sites. I read some of the displays and stopped in at the BLM visitor center to learn about steam boating and the Montana gold rush. But mostly I arranged for a pickup later that day by Jim Adkins to take me from there instead of the usual Carter Ferry, though they hardly ever dealt with somebody going upriver. Then I shopped for groceries, had the $6 pizza/salad buffet at Pizza Pro, and washed and dried my dirty clothes. With the rain and unknown phone service ahead, I had opted out of canoeing to Carter Ferry; good day to be inside.

#720 Jim Adkins with my load

Jim took me 43 miles to the Big Bend boat launch about 10 miles up from Great Falls. On the way, he showed me two of the dams, Giant Springs (visited by Lewis and Clark) and the Odd Fellows Park where most downstream canoes are picked up for portage. I could see that I would be missing some extreme exertion getting past the 5 falls and their dams; at some of the dams, most, if not all, of the current went underground to their power stations. With the rock walls of the canyons, Jim was pretty sure that you couldn't portage some of the dams. In fact Jim mentioned a German duo who tried it and he couldn't remember if they were ever heard from again. I possibly could have taken out at Morony dam and portaged on gravel roads for 20 miles and then through town for another 8 miles to Odd Fellows Park; this late in the trip and in the year, I would have chanced a single trip. But I wasn't sure I could even get out of the canyon there or which side of the canyon had a road or the best road. Besides I had committed to meeting my friend Mike at the Bozeman airport on October 5, a little more than 2 weeks away.

#721 One of the dams in Great Falls, on CD only

#722 Another dam, almost no water for canoes

#723 Portage point

That night I was serenaded by a Big Bend Orchestra–beaver tail slaps followed by a falling tree, geese mutterings and coyote howls in the background, punctuated by a owl's dog imitation morphing into a traditional whooing. Police visited me about midnight, asking my opinion on the orchestral performance and something about a No Camping sign I think. 47 miles, 4 by canoeing

Chapter 13

Cold Water Missouri

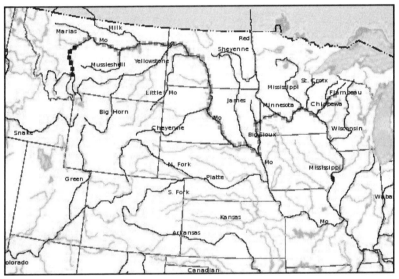

#724 Canoeing to the Missouri River Headwaters

Sunday, September 18. Dried things while I repacked the canoe and made oatmeal, off by 10:15 a.m. with south wind but going west with 3 oxbows. River current mellow compared to below Fort Benton. Saw what I believe were the first houses close to the Missouri since I started in Sioux City. Lots of geese. Saw 5 deer, including a 6 point buck. Paddled about 6 hours and sailed 2 hours on the oxbow legs going north. Took an hour hike to the south about a mile before camp where I had cell phone service. Saw 2 coyotes, a doe, a spike buck and 2 big 8 to 10 point bucks, all white tail deer, I think. This week has been good for wildlife, seeing lots of woodcock, sand hill cranes, pigeons using the cliffs, an osprey and a bald eagle. 6 miles

#725 Nice looking house, on CD only

#726 Scenery next door, on CD only

#727 Geese in flight

#728 Daisy eyeing deer, on CD only

#729 Hiking area, on CD only

#730 River view

#731 Mountain view, on CD only

#732 Twilight time on upper Mo, on CD only

Monday, September 19. Going west on average with a fierce southwest wind but not too bad near shore usually. I was able to sail 2 or 3 times for a half mile each time on the appropriate curves north. Stopped for a chicken and potato lunch at Ulm and also bought a Pepsi 12 pack and 4 candy bars. Saw lots of geese and ducks, 4 bald eagles, 2 of them immature. I wish I could identify hawks. 5 miles

#733 Morning mountains, on CD only

Tuesday, September 20. The average direction of the river just changed from west to southwest as I am going upstream and, though still curvy like all rivers, hardly any oxbows. Cordeled mostly, some paddling, a little sailing. Good wildlife again today--cormorants, pelicans, 6 deer, a coyote next to unconcerned cows, cranes, maybe my first golden eagle, though easily confused with immature bald eagles. Talked to a couple of guys fly fishing out of a doubly pointed skiff, catching trout "once in a while" 9 miles

#734 Butte from river

#735 Mountains, on CD only

Wednesday, September 21. Wind against me, so cordeled mostly, paddled some. Tried fishing with grasshoppers at about 2 p.m.; saw 11 and 15 inch trout but caught nothing; so napped. Scenery improved towards evening. Met JD and Colleen at my camp on Pelican Point as they finished a fishing float. Pelican Point was named by Lewis and Clark and had pelicans this day also. These are white pelicans and my Internet research and my observations agree that they don't dive like brown pelicans do in Florida; they dip their big bills (can hold 3 gallons) into the water and strain out fish. Sometimes they herd fish towards each other and dip out of the center. I never saw little pelicans as I did little geese, but Internet tells me they do breed up here in the north, west of the Great Lakes. Perhaps the young of these birds are like young eagles in that they don't leave the nest until they are as big as the adults.

Also at Pelican Point I talked with an outfitter, Jason, here to fish trout on his time off. 8 miles

#736 on CD only

#737 Pelicans on Pelican Point

#738 on CD only

#739 JD and Colleen

Thursday, September 22. Pelican Point was a busy place that morning; 11 vehicles were parked there when I left at 11 a.m. Had pancakes made from store-bought mix with similar syrup. Talked with Felicia and John who were biking back to Mountain Palace after canoeing.

#740 Hills, no trees

#741 Bigger hills with trees, on CD only

#742 Swimming deer, on CD only

#743 Canoe stern, beaver cache (?)

In the last picture I was mystified by the fresh pile of mud near shore. But the picture also shows the rudder mechanism well; note the rope holding the rudder in the up position and the large, rigid, easily accessible, square rudder handle.

At one fast and deep spot I had to empty the canoe and drag it over and between rocks closer to and on shore. A little later, at his invitation, I had a late lunch on the lawn of Ricardo Valdez from Colorado; he might be surprised some day to see a picture of his house in this book. Also waded at the first I-15 bridge, but was able to paddle up shore current after that. Shores were starting to tighten as I approached camp at Mountain Palace Recreational Area, just beautiful; the grey clouds and the setting sun enhanced the dark beauty of the rocks, but also under-developed most of my pictures. (The Atlas had this area misplaced; it should be placed further upstream 2 miles above the Hardy bridge.)

#744 House of Ricardo, on CD only

#745

#746 Rocky cliffs closing in, on CD only

#747 on CD only

I remet JD and Colleen and was treated to filet mignon, rice, salad and somores in their camper. This wonderful meal was the start of a 2 day gourmet foodfest (see Friday). Rained overnight. 3 miles

Friday, September 23. I put out a grasshopper as I was bailing the canoe and caught a 20 inch rainbow trout. I took 3 more pictures before and as I left camp. Rained all day, this night, and all the next day; a lot. And it was cold. My notes don't say, but I believe I used a mix of paddling and poddling as the shore was pretty steep and user unfriendly; I know I didn't get very far. I hid from the rain under an I-15 bridge and cooked my trout. The fish was great but the ambiance so-so.

#748 Ruler broken at 14 inches

#749 Big, on CD only

#750 Downriver, on CD only

#751 View back towards camp as leaving, on CD only

#752 on CD only

#753 Cordeling view, on CD only

#754 Interstate amidst houses and rocks, on CD only

Mid-morning I was hailed by Dane Lauman who invited me out of the rain into his house to meet his wife, Pat, drink cocoa, and eat Pat's home-made ginger snaps, a wonderful hour break. I gave Dane my two 9 mm, 30 inch long tent repair poles to hold up his antelope decoy.

#755

I camped at Mid Canon (Spanish for and pronounced like canyon) and met Dave McKee, a reputed author and Bozeman outdoor reporter who had no interest in my adventure; hey, he was on vacation. Ate the last of my cookies and bananas from Cascade shopping a couple of days before. Jack Crandall from Michigan stopped to talk as I was walking back from non-town Mid Canon and then returned the next day with 2 cans Dinty Moore, a roll of plastic bags, and 4 fruit cups, and said he would leave 20 pounds of dog food at the Craig Cross Currents Fly Shop. What a nice thing to do. I knew by this time that my back pack, where I kept my extra clothes, was not water-proof and I should have wrapped everything in plastic, but kept forgetting to buy bags. If my clothes were ever dry again, I'd use those bags.

Did I mention that it rained? All night. 4 miles

#756 Jack Crandall

#757 on CD only

#758 on CD only

Saturday, September 24. Everything wet except the top of my sleeping bag and the underwear I slept in. No supplies in Mid Canon or Craig, no dry firewood either, not that I felt like cooking. Rained all day. Picked up Jack's gift of dog food and dropped off the litter I'd been picking up at the Fly Shop in Craig. It stopped raining towards evening and I met Adam, Tim, and Shaun in camp at the Craig Recreation Area. I had waved to them earlier during the day on their float trip. They were fishing guides also, from Big Sky, fishing on the far upper Mo as their vacation, apparently the best trout fishing in the world. Adam gave me many yards of 6 pound test line for my small reel which didn't have enough line of any kind. They explained for me that these doubly pointed skiffs with oars in the middle were named McKenzie drift boats, presumably (I thought) because they were invented on the McKenzie River of Canada. They had high sides and easily room for three. (See picture #651)

INTERNET REALITY CHECK: No, it was named for boats used on the McKenzie River in Oregon, a tributary of the Willamette River. To have been invented on the longest river in Canada, they would have needed an "a" in their Mc.

They invited me over to play a round of Texas Holdem for pride. I was first man out, refusing to fold even with no cards; I've been reflecting on that ever since. 5 miles

Sunday, September 25. I could see snow on the foothills to the northeast. I dried things in the wind and sunshine until about noon. Made oatmeal, pudding, cocoa. Spent $4 for candy, root beer, and popcorn at Joe's cafe last night before playing cards; down to $5.75 in cash. Paid $7 in checks 3 times to Montana GF and Parks for camping lately; didn't pay Friday night because it was too wet to write a check. Packed up using plastic bags from Jack. Left about 1 p.m., waved to the poker players on another of their floats, happy to see bright sun and blue sky illuminated my life and the forested hillsides. Cordeled half the time and paddled the rest. Rocks were closing in as I approached camp at Holter dam. Treated to spaghetti and meat balls by fellow camper Linda from Hamilton, Montana. Paid $6 camp fee to BLM. Met Ken and Buck from north Idaho. 6 miles

#761 Snow in the distance

#762 Sun, I like it, on CD only

Monday, September 26 Made the third of a mile portage on the right in 2 carries by noon.

#763 Western Grebe, a diving bird like the loon, on CD only

#764 Mule deer seen on the portage, on CD only

#765 Holter dam

#766 View upwind on Lake Holter, on CD only

Fierce wind against me down the length of Holter Flowage, so made phone calls to brothers Jon and Joe. Hiking possibilities didn't look great so with a little less wind I paddled southeast right into it for a half hour to reach a point, a rest, and lunch. I tried following the more sheltered shore line to the right, but couldn't do it–to keep away from the shore I had to paddle continuously on the right and, too soon, my right arm gave out, and, without a change in tactics, I would have been blown into the shallows and waves. By going straight into the wind I could switch sides and keep going nearly indefinitely; well, longer. After reaching the point, I could see from the Atlas that I'd be sheltered from the wind for the rest of the day if I could make the next few miles. Five months of conditioning allowed me to paddle the 3 miles (by GPS) in 1.5 hours without stopping.

#767 Shelter

#768 Rare houses, on CD only

#769 Same site, view ahead, on CD only

#770 12 sheep, all small rams, I think

The wind was slowing continually so that it was no help when I got to the downwind leg of the oxbow at the end of the lake, but it was all much easier paddling with the steep sides as shelter and of course no current on the flowage. The shores closed in again in late afternoon. Close to camp time I met 3 guys from Helena who gave me one of their jumbo perch (a fat 13 inches), a 16 inch walleye, and a box of worms. They were fishing in really deep water, 30 feet and more I think. I tried that but had no luck, perhaps because I had no good anchor. I fished in 10 to 15 feet of water, threw back 2 small walleyes and kept 4 small perch, greedily eating them all up with a cup and a half of rice. 8 miles

#771 on CD only

#772

Tuesday, September 27. Windy all night and in the morning towards my direction of south, wind opposite of the day before. Made oatmeal and pancakes with 4 extra for lunch. Took a short hike near camp before leaving. The speed to scenery ration was way too high as I sailed through the Gates of the Mountains, but between the impending late Fall, high elevation cold (about 4000 feet here) and my goal of meeting Mike, I decided not to lower the sail. I think I managed to capture the magnificence of the place with my one-handed camera technique.

#773 Scarce meadow, on CD only

#774 Sailing into the Gates of the Rocky Mountains

#775 Rocky shore, on CD only

#776 Gates

#777 View past gate; proceed left I guess, on CD only

#778 View to right, on CD only

#779 View up left

#780 5 minutes later, on CD only

#781 Another gate, 17 minutes past the first gate, on CD only

#782 Same site, steep shore

#783 Inside the second gate, on CD only

#784 Badland character, on CD only

#785 Leaving the gates, on CD only

#786 Looking back

After the Gates, the wind increased and the canyon narrowed. I had to lower the sail and paddled only to steer, up fast rapids for 2 or 3 miles right to the bottom of Hauser dam–What a ride! But no time for pictures!

Wanting to milk this wind as much as possible, I hurried through the third of a mile right hand portage and continued my tail wind ride without sail for another 2 hours to camp on Lake Hauser. Had Raman noodles with veggies and pudding. 13 miles

Wednesday, September 28. Heavy frost, with ice in my water bottle. No wind but no current either as I paddled above the Hauser dam, past York (named for Lewis's slave) and all the way up to Canyon Ferry dam. BLM guys Roger, Don, Shawn, and Dave used their trucks to carry me 2 miles from Riverside campground to Court Sherriff campground on Canyon Ferry Lake, another great time-saver.

#787 View on Lake Hauser, on CD only

#788 Heron over shore, on CD only

#790 Roger, Jim, and Daisy at portage, on CD only

#791 Canyon Ferry Dam

#792 Mule deer doe on lake near marina, on CD only

I stopped briefly at Kim's Marina for bread and 2 candy bars and talked with some fellow sailors. I caught a deer hiding and took a picture coming out of the marina. I then paddled another 4 miles, exhausted. 14 miles

#793 Canyon Ferry Lake, on CD only

#794 Sunset, on CD only

#795 Seagulls and something bigger, probably pelicans

Thursday, September 29. Up and gone by 8:30. Having no wind nor current here on Canyon Ferry Lake, I timed myself and measured the distance with GPS as I paddled per usual. I did 4.5 miles in 1.5 hours, i.e. 3 miles an hour. I tried my hardest paddling once with the GPS on and got it up to 4 mph; Nate and I just touched 10 mph once in fast current on the Yellowstone. With breaks and lunch subtracted, I was good for about 6 hours of paddling. So if I ever had a calm day on a long lake, I could probably paddle about 18 miles and still enjoy it.

A LITTLE MORE: There is a generally accepted formula for the maximum speed (limited by friction) of a boat on calm water of length L feet at the water line, Max Speed in mph = 1.54 times the square root of L; for a 17 foot canoe, this comes to 6.35 mph.

Around 1 o'clock, I saw a herd of 10 antelope. As I lunched on the west side at Beaver Creek Boat Launch, a fierce wind came up from the south, the direction I was heading towards. So I fished without luck for an hour and then cordeled. Cordeling was tough because of the wind pushing the canoe to shore depending on wind and shore direction, because the bays were deep into the land but shallow in water depth, and because there were often big rocks along the shore. So I was much happier when the wind died and I could paddle in a straight line in deep water, even happier when a mild tail wind came up to help as I paddled. The wind died at the end of the lake and I pulled and cordeled through 2 miles of lake mud about 2 inches deep, then the same upriver with no mud for a half mile to the Highway 287 bridge park below Townsend. I walked into town for 3 hot dogs, soda, nachos, brownie, roll, and large Butterfinger. Good day, tired, glad I could buy supper. 17 miles

#796 Antelope, on CD only

#797 Evening view on Canyon Ferry Lake, on CD only

Friday, September 30. Townsend Ford dealer let me use an outlet to charge my cell phone and I talked with Mike to confirm October 5 and left a message for Jon. Back at camp I met Yutaka Tezuka on a 20 day fishing trip of the best fly fishing areas in North America. I also remet Roger and Don of the BLM, cleaning up the camp.

I left about 11:30 and found Yutaka on the river. As I watched him fish an eddy with a fly, he tied into and eventually caught a

#798 Don (left) and Roger at my camp

320

beautiful 10 pound carp, if carp are ever beautiful. In most of the eddies dirty foam accumulates and it looks like, and could be, floating cow manure; I assumed as I saw carp suck the surface that they were recycling the stuff. But somebody suggested that they were sucking down associated flies and maggots and thus could be caught on artificial flies; I guess that would make the

#799 Yutaka and carp

carp a secondary recycler rather than primary. Though it is holiday fare in Germany, we don't often eat carp in America, so I guess what carp eat is of no big concern. But just now I thought of the wonderful trout that are caught here–Do you suppose a hungry trout is picky about where he catches his fly or what he slurps down with it? I think maybe the cow shit should land elsewhere.

I was mostly cordeling in tennis shoes. I knew it was way too cold for rattlesnakes, but was confused when I saw a garter snake. As I was cordeling along what Lewis and Clark called the Crimson Bluffs, I stepped over and then went back to pick up what I still think are 2 special rocks. It was obviously at one time a single piece of sandstone that had split open as it fell, but who would have guessed the hidden beauty inside, as the pattern didn't extend more than an inch from the center of the pattern. I was able to split off half inch layers of stone on the outside of each piece to get the total weight down to about 9 pounds; glad I wasn't backpacking.

#801 Crimson Bluffs

#802 Where I picked up my rocks, on CD only

Encountered a fallen tree that made me challenge the current and observed that the cottonwood leaves were turning color. Saw about 4 mule deer. Lots of sounds overnight and early next morning–elk bugles, beaver slaps, cranes, geese, pheasants, ducks, coyotes, highway, railroad, owl, gunshots. Nice day. 7 miles

#803 Heart rocks in Wisconsin snow later

#804 Problems in cordeling, on CD only

#805 Fall coming, on CD only

Saturday, October 1. Took an early morning hour walk along a slough without current. Saw 4 elk cows and a 4x4 bull, 4 doe whitetail deer with a 6 or 8 point buck. Opening of waterfowl season for everything but cranes.

#806 Sunrise in the Rockies, on CD only

#807 Whitetail doe

I left about 9:30. There was some sparkle on the river as I left and pretty scenery as I cordeled.

#808 Sparkle, on CD only

#809

#810 Almost too shallow to cordle, on CD only

Saw 3 mule deer while cordeling. Wind came up strong enough to sail for about an hour, even up some fast rapids. As the wind blew harder, I lowered the sail and continued up the rapids just steering, as I did last Tuesday, all the way to the Toston dam. A fisherman helped me drag the lightened canoe to the road and then short wheelings to camp on Lake Toston. Picnickers intentionally left me some hot dogs and a big fire and accidentally left a Buck knife with blade embedded in the dirt. I cooked the hot dogs and also pudding on the fire. I met Debbie from Butte who works on Special Olympics. I gave her a working Zebco reel with broken rod along with a sandals I had found 30 miles apart but were now reunited, picking up the first one as litter; you never know. 9 miles

#811 Toston dam, on CD only

#812 Back together, on CD only

#813 Camp on pretty Lake Toston

#814 Larry (left) and Mr. Pintail

Sunday, October 2 Rained a quarter inch overnight. Made pancakes, dried stuff, talked with Larry and another hunter whose real name I missed but whose license plate called him "MRPINTAIL". They showed me a shoveler, American widgeon, and a gadwall they had shot and offered them to me.

Then just before I left at about 12:30, I talked with another pair of duck hunters who were enthralled with the idea of my trip; I gave them my web site, sistersfarm.com, but never heard from them. I sailed for a half mile going west on the first leg of a long oxbow, then paddled on the lake for a far too short 3 miles and cordeled against medium current among rocks that varied in size from marbles to footballs, i.e. hard walking, cold, and wet to my thighs. Saw bald eagles with their black-headed young. Tried fishing with grasshoppers but no luck. 7 miles

#815
#816 Fall on the lake, on CD only

#817 Railroad and cave, on CD only

#818 Abandoned railroad bridge

#820 Looking back the Little Gates of the Rockies area, on CD only

#821 Looking ahead to snow and the Three Forks Basin

Monday, October 3. Rained a quarter inch again overnight, and then rained half the day. Cordeled almost all day, no wind, no sun, cold, wet to knees all day. Saw about 30 ducks, hardly any other wildlife except a beaver and lots of beaver sign. Nice canyon area, rocky but not as hard to walk as yesterday. Lots of trains on the east side, abandoned on the west side. Engineers would toot as I waved. Passed a quarry and cement plant (Trident) a mile below Three Forks Park but I didn't realize that I was that close.

I, of course, had figured that all three forks of the Missouri would come in at the same place, but actually the junction between the Jefferson from the west with the central Madison is about a half mile above their junction with the Gallatin from the southeast. The Madison was a lot bigger than the Gallatin which seemed a lot bigger than the Jefferson, in volume and width.

I drifted back down to the junction with the Gallatin, in a bit of a daze not being ready to be done and slowly realizing I had no obvious goal anymore. I came up the Gallatin a couple of hundred yards to a site across from Headwaters State Park. As my head settled some and I realized I had done it, actually paddled from my back yard well into the Rocky Mountains (only 50 miles from the Continental Divide), I eagerly climbed the ridge to the east which ended in a fine observation point at its southern end to get a good view of the place. This was surely, as I read later, the same ridge that Lewis climbed with probably the same excitement. I took several pictures of the big bowl to the east, south, and a little west, noting the snow on the mountains to the east and southeast. Good phone service applied as you might expect and I made several calls and a picture of a passing train as I descended back to the canoe. The visibility was not great this day, so I came back 3 days later with Mike and took more pictures.

#822 View overlooking junction of Gallatin with other two

#823 Gallatin valley

#824 Up Jefferson Valley

#827 BN&SF again, on CD only

#829 More sun

#831

#833, on CD only

I had left home 175 days before. Adding up all the camp-to-camp GPS miles came to 1744 miles, with 1194 of those on the Missouri. These 1194 miles would correspond with 1602 river miles, since Three Forks is officially at 2341 and Sioux City at 739 river miles. Assuming this same ratio applies to the rivers between Ladysmith and Sioux City, I calculate a total of 2399 river miles, about the same as if I had started in St. Louis. Disregarding the 4 days I didn't canoe gives an average of 10.2 camp-to-camp GPS miles and 14.0 river miles per day. At Three Forks I was 984 miles from home, GPS or tired crow.

I had canoed pretty hard from 9:30 to 4:30 and found a suitable camp site in the park. I hardly got any sleep as both feet were red, swollen, and tender to the ankles from wading in the water for days–I hadn't realized there was more to forebear than just toughing out the cold. The weight of the sleeping bag was too much on my toes, yet it was too cold without the bag. 7 miles

Tuesday, October 4. Since the East Gallatin passed close to the airport about 20 miles upstream, one option seemed to be to canoe close to and portage right to the airport, but the Gallatin was too swift and shallow to paddle, too swift and gravelly to poddle, I was afraid to get my feet wet and cold again if I cordeled, and no wind to sail. I only cordeled about a half mile to figure this out and floated back to camp. Around noon I called Bim Fischer, a friend and co-worker of Jon, who picked me up after work at about 4:30; I walked after 2:30 to stay warm and saw the park and its displays several times. Bim filled me with pizza, comforted me with a warm bed and house, and helped me wash and dry all my clothes. 0 miles

Chapter 14

Wyoming and Colorado

Wednesday, October 5. I left Daisy at Bim's for the day and Bim dropped me off in the town of Belgrade. I bought 3 pair of pants at Sacks Thrift Shop, used the library to catch up on email and to read most of Jack Horner's book on dinosaur bones in Montana, mailed a small camera and exposed film to the Zieslers who had been giving pictures to the Ladysmith News, and walked 2 miles to the airport to meet Mike at about 7 p.m. on his flight from Chapel Hill, North Carolina.

#833 View of the airport and north, on CD only

Mike Su (alias Ying Fu Su, son of a Japanese father and a Taiwanese mother) had come to Montana State in Bozeman from Taiwan in the late 1960s for graduate school in the only field available, entomology. He achieved a master's degree there, loving Montana and America, and was working on a Ph. D. in pharmacology in Denver when I was a post-doc there at the University of Colorado Medical Center. We both moved with Dr. John Perkins when he became chairman of the Department of Pharmacology at the University of North Carolina in Chapel Hill; our families were very close. I had told him about my trip plans and he guffawed that, were I to actually do that, he would come welcome me at the other end. I did and so he did. He was looking forward to and did enjoy seeing Bozeman and Montana again.

We rented an economical Chevy Cobalt, toured Bozeman's down town, ate pizza, and slept at Bim's house. 0 miles, but warm

Thursday, October 6. Mike and I loaded up the car with camp gear, food, and dog. Then we saw more of Bozeman and the College, made 2 photo CDs at WalMart and sent one to Polly, shopped there for food, and then started driving towards Glacier National Park. We had a pleasant drive to Mountain Palace, my previous and favorite mountain camp site where I had caught my only trout. I tried fishing with a fly without luck.

#834 Fisherman along Mo

#835 Mike and Cobalt

#836 3x3 mulie, on CD only

#837 Mountain Palace, my tent

Friday through Tuesday, October 7-11 We drove north to Glacier National Park, seeing antelope on the way and bear, deer, and elk in the park.

#838 We assumed the rainbow was a Park gimmick

#839 Black bear, on CD only

#840 St. Mary's Lake in Glacier

Snow had already blocked the Going to the Sun Road, but we did see St. Mary's Lake. We camped at 2 Medicine Lake where I led Mike on an evening hike around the lake, enjoyable for 2.5 hours but lasted for 3. We encountered Paradise Creek where the authorities had removed the planking from the bridge for the winter and neglected to tell us in sign language back at the trailhead. It was too far and we were too tired to turn back, and it was getting dark, so we waded the fast, icy water up to our knees. We felt lucky that we didn't slip and get totally wet. I see now that it was at least a 5 mile hike; Mike was in good shape for being 63; I was only 60.

#841 Two Medicine Lake, on CD only

Saturday we drove west across the Continental Divide and along Highway 2 to Kalispell, then south through Missoula and Butte, then back across the Divide, staying in a Three Forks motel, the Lewis and Clark Lodge. Sunday we picked up more gear for my Colorado camping from Bim's garage, drove through Yellowstone Park past Old Faithful, seeing buffalo, deer and elk, though the best activity was observing all the people who came to see Yellowstone–all ages, nationalities, languages, sizes–what a species we are! We camped at the Signal Mountain camp site in Grand Teton National Park.

#843 Yellowstone buffalo

#844 An amazing species at Old Faithful

#845 Grand Tetons (No, "Great Heads" don't come in pairs), on CD only

#846 Next day; but they really are grand!

#847 Moose in the swamp, on CD only

Monday morning, October 10 We searched the map more carefully this time and found a short hike to Phelps Lake overlook, enjoyable for the full 2 hours, seeing 2 moose on the road to the trailhead. We then drove south through Rock Springs and followed Wyoming 430 which turned into Colorado county road 10 and camped 30 miles further in Irish Canyon.

#848 Phelps Lake, on CD only

#849 Irish Canyon, on CD only

#850 Irish Canyon, Colorado

Tuesday we took a short hike in this striking canyon, looking for shed antlers but finding none. Reaching Colorado Highway 318 we drove back northwest thinking we could enter Dinosaur National Park from the north. We were wrong but enjoyed the scenery around Browns Park National Wildlife Refuge and especially Brown's Park store with its friendly owners and very reasonable prices on the groceries and treats we bought. Then we drove back southeast almost to Maybell near where Jon hunts rabbits (170 of them in 2007 when the rabbits were eating themselves out of habitat) and where I shot my only antelope years ago. Then we found some backroads south to Highway 40 and east to the Park's Visitor Center and camped at the Green River campground amidst impressive scenery.

#851 The Gates of the Green River

#852 Dinosaur Park, on CD only

Wednesday we toured the Center and especially the hill side quarry enclosed inside, showing petrified dinosaur bones sticking out of the dirt. Then we drove south to the town of Dinosaur and Rangely (where we forgot to buy gas), past the Book Cliffs and Parachute Creek where I was introduced to Colorado through bow and arrow mule deer hunting, and Grand Junction where we happily drove into a gas station. We took the backway through Paonia, buying some of the wonderful West Slope pears, plums, and peaches (though it was way past peach time and these peaches were lousy) and over McClure Pass, through Carbondale to Jon's house in Basalt, downriver from Aspen on the Roaring Fork. Brothers Jon and Joe and friend Jay had taken camp equipment up Avalanche Creek this day to about 8700 feet with Jay's horses; Joe had remained for the night.

Thursday, Mike left for Denver via the scenic and slow Independence Pass through Aspen and Leadville. He visited some friends in Denver and left me the car at the airport long term parking lot. Jon and I, carrying only light packs, took the 2 horses into camp also lightly loaded with food and more equipment, a 4.5 hour hike. Jay and our friend Dave from Iowa came in by 6 pm.

On Friday everybody went up higher, without horses, to about 10,000 feet to be in position for the gun bull elk hunt starting the next morning. There were already about 10 inches of snow in the shade up that high. I helped Jon and Joe pack their stuff up there and then came back down to base camp to feed the horses. Daisy walked with me pretty well; she didn't chase any elk or show me a bear cub in a tree like she did the year before.

Saturday through Thursday, Everybody had a good time hunting, hiking, observing, eating. I was leaving foot prints all over the mountains during the day between pasturing the horses morning and evening. Jon's scale indicated that I had lost 30 pounds, down to 185 and I felt great after my red blood cell count kicked up to adjust to the altitude. Jay figured after canoeing 5 months, I would be able to "walk up to camp on my hands", but I never could balance well that way, much less carry a pack. Jon and Joe both missed shots at 4x4 bulls (the minimum required for this season) but they had gotten bulls that size before; and, perhaps because of these misses, they each shot 6x6 bulls the next year which they mounted. We came out elkless but still heavily loaded, horses and men, on Thursday to enjoy Jon's wife Ronda's elk stew at Jon's house. I borrowed a canoe paddle I had made for Jay years before, knowing my son Nate would need one.

#854 View from trail up Avalanche Creek

#855 Camp in Upper Dooly Meadow

#856 Jon (left), Jim, Joe

#857 Jay Halliday (left) and Dave Anderson

Friday, October 21. Dave picked me up at 4 a.m. and dropped me off at the rental car in the Denver airport on his way back to Iowa. I drove to Thermopolis, Wyoming, enjoying the expansive scenery with antelope and deer and slept in the car. Saturday I had time for a slow ride to Cody, with side trips, to pick up Nate around noon, flying in from El Paso via Salt Lake City; he was living then in Las Cruces, New Mexico, 50 miles north of El Paso. We drove through Yellowstone and camped on Rob Story's land near Emigrant. Rob had a fire going for us in the woods near his home on the old homestead. We conversed by the fire, Nate and Rob obviously enjoying each other's wit and stories. Later, Nate and I chuckled about how Rob wished that, for some of his projects, he could have hired the PR man that the porcupine species evidently hired to spread the thought that one shouldn't kill porkies wantonly in case you ever had to club one when you were starving.

#858 A Yellowstone Park stream

Sunday, October 23. We had breakfast with Rob, Colleen and their 2 kids and then Rob showed us the canoe launch site. Nate and I then made more use of our $20 Yellowstone pass by touring the western side of Yellowstone, seeing Old Faithful, again for me, first time for Nate, as well as other Yellowstone scenery and sites. Then we drove back to Three Forks area where I showed Nate that park. Then to Bim's house and spent the night there. Georgia fixed us a late night supper of delicious leftovers.

#859 Back for a picture at Headwater State Park

Chapter 15

The Yellowstone

#860 Canoeing The Yellowstone River back to North Dakota

Monday, October 24. We loaded Bim's truck with canoe and gear and he met us with it at the airport after I returned the rental car. He dropped us off at Rob's put-in by about 9:15; it would have been hard to accomplish this portage without Bim, besides the great, warm hospitality–nice guy!

Nate and I caught and ate 3 trout for breakfast (the last fish I caught on the trip) along with pancakes and then canoed a long way downriver with some class 2 rapids. Not a good time to make a mistake because we had 700 pounds of weight plus canoe; but we were strong, we kept talking to each other about paths through the water, and the water was just deep enough, with the occasional scraping over sand and gravel. Wonderful day, temperature in the 60s and great scenery. 10 miles

#861 Trying out my new boots, on CD only

#862 Nate

#863 Yellowstone River Scenery in October

#864 Active beaver, on CD only

Tuesday, October 25. After a nice morning float on a nice day with a nice lunch and a beaver sighting, we found a Class 2 rapids with Class 4 consequences as we screwed up. We had agreed on right at the beginning of the chute and then both thought differently about what was obvious after that, without talking. The canoe floated sideways into a protruding log.

We spent the afternoon drying out and retrieving stuff that floated and stuff that sunk. Nate swam down in about 5 feet of faster water for sunken stuff we could barely see; I don't think I could have made myself go under that cold water. There was a shallow hot spring just off shore to warm up in. We lost Nate's glasses, the light-duty fishing pole and reel, and some clothes that were drying at the time. And the canoe was way out of shape. Bummer.

#865 Post dump

After stomping out the bottom of the canoe, we discussed how to seal the 3 cracks near the floor of the canoe. We had rivets, drill, drill bits, and hammer. I found some thin steel off of a car and we had the galvanized steel flashing of the wind shield for the cook stove. We didn't have good gasket material, except maybe my new rubber boots. 8 miles

Wednesday, October 26. We decided to try sealing the cracks with the fabric tape I had brought along for sail patching, and it held nicely even with the canoe fully loaded. About this time Roy Senter and friend George floated by in their drift boat and told us where to take out in Livingston. We canoed without problem and no serious leaks to the first boat launch on the left in Livingston. We put all our stuff in Roy's boat already on his trailer and brought our stuff and me downriver a mile to Mayor's Landing Park. Then Roy unloaded his boat at his home, picked up Nate and the canoe, and brought the canoe to Livingston Welding. 2 miles

Thursday, October 27. I had bent the rudder sometime during the trip, so with some spare time, I hiked into town and found Jim at Mobile Welding willing to make time to straighten it and also make me a stainless steel pin to mount the rudder; I had gone through about 4 aluminum tent stakes as weak pins. Jim did both jobs right away for just $14.

Roy, George, and Roy's girl friend Ruth brought us the canoe in early afternoon, welded nicely for $40. Roy wrote a story for my first book on his life story and especially on fly fishing on the Yellowstone.

Because of cracks in both rear gunnels, the canoe floated a little low on the right front and left rear, but worked well. 18 miles

#866 on CD only

#867 on CD only

Friday, October 28. No notes for the day. I had bought a $130 pheasant license for Nate, so he and Daisy were occasionally walking fields as I canoed, but they found no pheasants this way. 25 miles

#868 Looking for pheasants

#869 Nate trying to steer as I use the camera, on CD only

Saturday, October 29. Cool day that turned rainy later; I spent a lot of time at the end of the day in a laundromat in Columbus drying clothes and me. I talked to John Mahonen who was an electrician at the local platinum mine. Meanwhile Nate was cooking a great noodles and cheese dish with morel mushrooms from Rob Story. He was doing this under a windy shelter in the park as he cussed the wet wood and the wood stove for not burning hot enough. Later that night he threw it all up and I had diarrhea. 22 miles

Sunday, October 30. Scenery particularly engaging today.

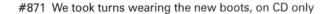

#871 We took turns wearing the new boots, on CD only

#872

#873

I camped at Laurel while Nate was picked up by friends he had known at Williams College in western Massachusetts. There was a collection center at the Laurel park of deer and elk heads for analysis on their brains for CWD, Chronic Wasting Disease. This is a mysterious (prion-caused) brain disease that, unlike Mad Cow Disease, hasn't been found in humans. It slowly kills deer and elk in Montana and Colorado, and now has been found in Wisconsin, probably through animals imported to game farms from the western states, a fine example of business "self-regulation." 24 miles

#874 Eagle landing

Monday, October 31. Had a high energy breakfast of peanut butter, bread, and Kool-Aid. Paddled hard so that I'd have time to rent a car in Billings.

#875 on CD only

#876 Detroit riprap

#877 on CD only

Had one harrowing experience near Billings where the canoe ground to a halt on a submerged rock in deep current as I was crossing the river. The left side dipped and started taking in water. I took a quick guess at the river depth, mostly hoped, and jumped in on the right side with my hand on the gunnel to right the boat. I was thrilled and chilled to feel my feet hit at about waist high and was able to righten the canoe and pull it off the rock. I pulled out soon after at a city boat landing and park in view of the I-90/94 bridge in east Billings. I quickly changed into dry clothes.

I met Gene, the acting superintendent of parks and used his cell phone to contact Nate as my cell phone was non-functional after our shipwreck. (Though it recovered later and I still use it.) We hid the canoe and sail in the bushes and put everything else in the big trunk of the rented Impala. We drove south and then east near Forsythe, looking for pheasants and hunting land but found neither. We slept in the car.

Tuesday, November 1. We kept driving east until we saw a rooster on the road near Forsythe and got permission to hunt on Jodi Steiger's land near there and bordering the river. I cooked bacon and potatoes and dried our clothes while Nate and Daisy hunted. He took 2 shots at a rooster, probably missed the first shot and the second was a dud, probably due to wet ammunition. Nate gathered the dried clothes but didn't notice my new pants and long underwear bottoms that had dried and blown off the propane tank.

We left the Forsythe area and investigated the area to the north, finding some really back roads I'll never see again. Ended up coming through Roundup seeing lots of deer and antelope, then through Billings and sleeping the night at the Cody airport.

#878 Sense of humor here; ranks with "Futility Farm"

#879 Standard backroad rental jeep on standard backroad, on CD only

Wednesday, November 2 We overslept a little and were at the back of the line for the 6:05 a.m. flight, and when they bumped 4 people to lighten the load because of high wind, Nate was one of them, as were Earl and Bob. All four of us drove back to Billings for a 10:30 flight to Salt Lake City.

I said good-bye to Nate, dumped nearly all of my belongings in the retrieved canoe, returned the car, and was then dropped off by Gordan of the rental agency. After he left I realized that my favorite paddle was still stuck up high in the trunk (where I had put it). My cell phone was working again so I was able to call the agency and beg them to return, which they did, graciously. I gave Gordan one of my postcards and a big Belgian chocolate bar which Nate and I had found again in the local WalMart.

Finally on the water again by 2 p.m., the weather was overcast and cold but I stayed warm by paddling hard against the wind but with that glorious current until 6 p.m. I portaged my first diversion dam on the left, a short 20 yards, about 6 feet of drop. 22 miles

#880 Rare waterfall, on CD only

#881 on CD only

#882

#883 Black birds, enough for pie

Thursday, November 3. Paddled from 9 to 6. I am very sensitive to the weather, especially cold, these days; the morning overcast turned to sun and wind in the afternoon, still cool but I could dry my pants as I wore them. I paddled to Pompey's Pillar for a short tour and lunch. You may remember that Pompey was the Lewis and Clark's nickname for Sacajawea's infant boy. Clark's chiseling of his name here is the only physical remnant of their trip, if one discounts the similar signature along the Missouri in 1805, "chiseled" in the sand of 2005 (picture #451).

#885 Pompey's Pillar

#886 Clark's signature, on CD only

#887 Clark's has the padlock, on CD only

#888 Rough shore, on CD only

I took a short hike on this pretty day. I sailed about 24 miles to the Custer bridge, then paddled another 5 miles more. River not as curvy as usual here. Scenery nice, but similar to the upper Missouri; fun going down hill. 34 miles

#889 View back upriver

#890 View downriver, ahead, on CD only

#891 on CD only

#892 on CD only

Friday, November 4. River curvy again. Saw a pretty red fox along the shore and lots of bald eagles with young. I was able to sail about 2/3 of the time, but fickle wind midday. Portaged 2 more diversion dams, both on the north side. Brad and Dana from Colstrip helped me line the canoe through a channel around the second dam. Camped at dark a little above Steiger's irrigation system. 29 miles

#893 Relentless river

#894 on CD only

Saturday, November 5. Took a sunrise hike over to Steiger's house and retrieved my pants and underwear; saw pheasants but no shots. I didn't feel guilty about hunting without a license as I had paid mightily for Nate's 1 shot. Saw a mink in the water that dove to get away. Spent almost 3 hours in Forsythe hiking in and out, shopping, and relaxing. Bought plastic gloves and Northridge Gardens hand cream for my skin, especially the backs of my hands. The cream came recommended and I agree that it

#895 Trent Thomas (right) and friend

is good stuff; I still have a little. Also bought another sponge, bananas, sweets. I think there were 2 diversion dams in Forsythe and after I returned from town, Trent trucked me around both of them.

#896 Hands, on CD only

I had a fair wind in the afternoon. Saw a herd of 10 deer; hunters in motor boat had 1 deer. Also saw an estimated 2000 Canada geese; counted 6 mature and 6 immature bald eagles. Good day to be on a river. 25 miles

Sunday, November 6. Was able to sail about half the time, but wind not great; current, however, was. Saw only 1 pheasant, lots of geese again, another 12 eagles and 2 flocks of turkeys, about 8 in each flock. I had hoped that I would keep my feet dry in my new rubber boots, but my toes, big toes especially, were so tender that the tops were blistering as they rubbed the boot tips. So I took off my boots in the canoe, my socks sometimes got wet and my feet stayed cold, wet or dry, in the shade of the canoe sides. Didn't get much sleep Friday or Saturday, but toes and hands were better this day. Found some pleasant scenery. Went past Miles City, camped near Matthews Recreation Area. 33 miles

#897 Turkeys

#898 on CD only

#899 on CD only

#900 Making hay

Monday, November 7. Wind little or brisk against me all day.
Saw another 10 eagles. My right shoulder was starting to hurt
some. Encountered a rapids that extended across the whole river;
could have been a real problem, but I found a chute. Powder
River entered from the south and muddied the rest of the water
ever after. Towards dark a homeowner near Terry greeted me and
invited me to camp in the next half mile on his land, but I went a
couple of miles further. The Yellowstone is now flowing northeast
on its journey to reach the Missouri . I was attempting to calculate
how many days to Williston so I could tell Kevin and Ian when to
pick me up. Using my plastic ruler that kept breaking smaller, I
estimated 120 miles GPS. If I continued to make 33 miles a day
this would be 4 days minimum, i.e. Friday. 33 miles

#902 Cable car to cross river, on CD only

#903 Two eagles, on CD only

#904 Good time for a nap, on CD only

#905 Abandoned railroad bridge near Miles City

#906 Dry scenery, on CD only

#907 Sunset, on CD only

Tuesday, November 8. Ugly day, light rain, gusty wind. Only 2 hours sleep last night. Both big toes had shooting pains about every 30 seconds. The weather cleared up in a "Big Sky" way with an obvious separation line at about 4 p.m.; I've never seen anything close to that before. I passed through Glendive without stopping. Lots of geese again, but also ducks today, flocks of 100. 37 miles

#909 Fast current, on CD only

#910 Slimmer canoe load these days, sailing

#911 Cloud line, on CD only

#912 Ditto, same time, more right

Wednesday, November 9. Took a diversion dam on the right, carried contents (a lot easier now than 7 months ago) and wheeled the canoe about 50 yards. Delightful day, cool but clear, wind with me and brisk. My GPS implied that I was sailing at 6-8 mph, sometimes 9. Saw pheasants, eagles, ducks, geese, white tail deer including a 4x4 in river. Passed by the town of Savage. The shores were back to mostly mud; river curvy this day, probably why my mileage was down a bit; didn't care as long as the sun shined. 27 miles

#913 on CD only

#914 on CD only

Thursday, November 10. Another wonderful day, warmer than yesterday but with a good wind also. Tried pheasant hunting twice for 2 hours and missed a couple of shots; Daisy is pretty good on pheasants. Toes still hurt as I walk but slept without pain for first time last night, though I still claimed I wasn't sleeping well. Passed by Sidney to the west, seeing lots of ducks. Ran out of water so boiled 2 quarts, mostly for cocoa. Also fried up reconstituted dried eggs that Nate had left me, tasted good.

Using up the buffalo jerky by feeding Daisy with it along with dog food. Camped in North Dakota. 26 miles

#915 About 200 ducks, on CD only

#916 Old lift bridge, bridging land

#917

#918 About 100 geese, on CD only

Friday, November 11. Veteran's Day A third good day in a row, possibly high 60s, but without my companion tail wind . Paddled to the Cartwright bridge (Highway 200) and then to the Confluence. Many boats fishing there for walleyes with good success, but mostly small fish I think. Had a nice lunch at the Center courtesy of my "old" friends Diane and Kim; got much needed water.

I watched a video on World War Two with about 4 vets and their wives from 2 to 3 p.m. I tried to thank them for what they and their slain comrades did for us and our world, but I did it poorly; I couldn't keep my eyes dry and my voice steady as I was mentally comparing my happy, vigorous float trip on the safe waters of the USA with the lifeless young corpses floating off of a Normandy beach. I haven't the words to properly condemn the self- or ethnic-centered stupidity of some male humans.

I paddled another 5 miles to the sand bar where I camped on the way up. No mosquitoes this time, no urine kept in the tent. Found one of my lost tent stakes. 12 miles, but with all the curves here it was more like 22 river miles.

#919 Old campsite, like an old friend

Saturday, November 12. Rain started at midnight, heard banks caving in all night, as Lewis and Clark did also. Did I mention I was camped on a SAND bar? I canoed in the rain all day from 9 a.m. to 1:15 p.m., paddling hard to keep warm; my wonderful Columbia rain jacket had lost its waterproofing and I was wet everywhere except my feet. The current wasn't much help and the wind was hard against me the last 4 miles.

Good day to quit, 7 months since April 13. I was shaking for an hour or more as I changed into dry clothes under a shelter at the Lewis and Clark Wildlife Management Area on the south side of the Highway 85 bridge, southwest of Williston. Kevin was in Fargo at 4:30 p.m. After I warmed up, I tried riveting a piece of sheet steel over the break in the left rear of the canoe to reshape it from a squat boat back to a more traditional type of canoe, but it didn't work. (After a run-in with a snowplow in 2006, I stripped it of seats, rudder bracket, and thwarts and sold it for $32.)

Kevin and Ian arrived after dark. 13 miles, curvy

#920 Rescued by Kevin and Ian Smith

Sunday, November 13. I was able to thank Kevin in person for taking care of my mail and bills over the last 7 months. We went south from Williston on U.S. 85, seeing the scenery of the Little Missouri Grasslands and of Theodore Roosevelt National Park, then east on I-94 through Bismarck, south on Highway 83, stopping at the old home of Lawrence Welk, and finally to Eureka, South Dakota. We rented a house there and hunted pheasants without success on Monday and Tuesday, though Daisy ran down a non-flying rooster. Arrived back in Ladysmith Wednesday, November 16. Glad I went, glad to be back.

SUMMARY:

27 fish meals for $170 of licenses, *a mere $7 per meal*

Total camp-to-camp GPS miles of trip to Three Forks plus Emigrant to Williston, *2162 miles*

Total calculated river miles at a ratio of 1.342 to 1, *2901 miles* (See end of Chapter 13 for source of ratio)

Furthest GPS distance canoed away from home, 3 Forks, *984 miles*

Time spent on trip, April 13 to November 12, *7 months* (with about 19 days traveling elsewhere, October 5-23)

Pounds lost: 215 minus 185, *30 pounds*

Number of pictures taken, *2105 pictures*

Acts of kindness encountered, *nearly uncountable*

Length of time before Daisy got bored and left me after trip, *2 months*

Pounds regained, *25 pounds*

Time before my first heart attack, *8 months*

Appendix 1

Equipment

The canoe was a 17 foot Grumman Eagle with a Grumman lateen sail package consisting of a 45 square foot sail, a 6.5 foot mast, 10 foot boom and gaff spar, a rudder assembly, and 2 wooden lee boards with an associated bracket that spanned the canoe just aft of the mast. I replaced the thwart behind the front seat with an oak thwart to provide a hole to support the mast at thwart level. The hole was lined with a large rubber grommet and the square end of the mast was seated in a square indent in the mast step attached to the bottom of the canoe. The mast grommet and step were obtained from Chicagoland Canoe Base, (312) 377-1489.

Because the Eagle ends do not curl back like most canoes, the rudder support had to be custom fit by a good machinist (Erle Barber in my case). Rather than use ropes to turn and hold the rudder, I bolted a tubular piece of lawn chair steel onto the rudder ears (See Picture #743). In this picture one can see the eighth inch rope used to lift the bottom of the rudder in shallow water or when not using the rudder. Because I was so heavy in the water, part of the rudder was always in the water; I came to lean back on the handle or fix it in place with a small rope when paddling. I fastened a pulley (or block in sailor lingo) to the oak thwart just to the left of the mast to allow the sail hoisting rope (halyard) to reach the pulley built into the top of the mast and then down to the gaff spar at about 4.5 feet from its junction with the boom. The sail is pictured and the mechanics of using it is discussed in Chapter 9 (Picture #470); some comments on sailing are offered early in the same chapter.

The wood burning cook stove (Picture #008, shown with a 13x33 inch wind shield made from galvanized steel flashing–heavy is good!) was a Sierra Zip, ordered through Campmore. Firewood was small enough to break by hand in order to fit inside the stove; When I had room in the canoe, I would store dry firewood in a covered pail. Charcoal works also.

The GPS was a Garmin Etrex.

The camera was a digital Pentax Optio33WR, 3.2 Megapixel, 2.8 zoom, water resistant.

The cell phone was an LG with Verizon service.

Favorite saw was a curved Gerber, Exchange-a-Blade (Picture #116).

Paddle was home-made from white ash, 4.5 feet long, 5.5 inches wide, weight 2.5 pounds.

Maps were Delorme Atlases.

Portage cart was of sturdy tubular steel construction with two 16 inch bicycle wheels. Its history is murky and I can't find a brand name on it. You can Google portage carts. One that sounds good is home-made in Ontario, sold by Bill Mungall, email: wmungall0809@rogers.com; in 2008 his price was only $80 plus shipping.

Tools carried were vice grips, adjustable wrench, small hack saw, hand drill with bits, ball peen hammer with rivets, inner tube repair kit and air pump (get a good one!), extra rope, screws, bolts, fabric tape good for tents, sails, canoes etc.

Appendix 2

Wood-fired Camp Cooking

Chocolate tapioca pudding: Stir together with a fork one egg, 1/4 cup granulated tapioca, 1/3 cup cocoa powder, 7/8 cup sugar, slowly add .5 cups milk while stirring with a flat-ended spatula, add 2 cups milk, bring to boil while stirring with the spatula so the pudding doesn't burn. Add nuts if you have them.

Fry bread: First make a bread dough that occupies less than half of a container with a lid. I used about 2 cups white flour, 1 cup rye flour, 1 cup whole wheat flour, .5 cup oat bran, .5 cup sugar, 1 Tablespoon dry yeast, stirring in enough drinking water to make a dough. Cover in a safe place through the day or overnight until it doubles in size or so. Now how does a camper make a pancake from a sticky hunk of fermented dough? He tears off a hunk of dough with his fingers (knowing any finger germs will get fried along with the dough), licks his fingers, then sprinkles an upside-down aluminum plate liberally with flour, and rolls the dough flat with his plastic, family-size, flour-dusted peanut butter jar, and cooks it with a little oil in a fry pan on top of a wood-burning stove. Then he hides it from black dogs.

Oatmeal: 1 cup dry oatmeal into 2 cups water; add brown sugar, nuts.

Oat cakes: Mix dry oatmeal with flour 1:1, add 1 teaspoon baking powder per cup of mix. Great with maple syrup.

Regular pancakes: Mix a teaspoon of baking powder with each cup of flour. Pancake mix is great also. I like nuts in all my pancake recipes.

Sour dough pancakes: I used a large Tupperware container with a so-so lid. Mix white flour and drinking water with the remnants of sour dough in the container from last time to a thick paste; it gets thinner as it works through the day. If it is too thick it may bubble out of the container and make a real mess in a backpack; if too thin it may leak out; i.e. damn stuff leaks. Pour or spoon it onto an oiled fry pan; turn it once. Eat with syrup or jam. Leave at least a half cup for starter. Keep a pill container of starter as a back-up; it stays viable for at least 3 years at room temperature.

Cocoa drink: .5 cup cocoa powder, 1 cup sugar, 1 cup dried milk into 3 cups hot water; cold water works too, stir longer, don't be fussy.

Mushrooms: It is fairly easy to identify the mushrooms I know since all of them are unique–get a book. Learn to identify the really poisonous mushrooms, the amanitas, and don't pick anything like them. There is always a chance of being wrong, don't mix mushroom types, cook up the whole batch, but taste only a forkful. Wait 2 hours and try 2 forkfuls; eat the rest the next day. These are the ones I eat: red chanterelle, oyster when it is on a tree or log, morels and false morels, honey, shaggy mane inky caps anytime and inky cap looking mushrooms that show some ink already. I think the only two of these with no chance of being poisonous are the oyster on a log or tree and the shaggy mane. I cut them into small pieces, fry them in margarine or olive oil and add a scrambled egg towards the end or as you rewarm them. Better than a dessert.

Soups and stews: I usually start with 3 cups water and add a cup of dried vegetables right away. After it is boiling add the noodles from a Raman package and, if wanted, cous cous or minute rice and less dried vegetables. Boil 3 minutes or so, remove from heat, and add the flavoring packet. If you want some meat, add small pieces of jerky or fresh fish along with the veggies. Make your own dried veggies with an electric dehydrator.

Spaghetti: Cook your noodles about 10 to 15 minutes in a small amount of boiling water; make hot cocoa with the excess water. Buy small plastic bottles of ready-made sauce; extra sauce should keep for 2 days. Try small pieces of jerky in with the noodles. Mac and cheese is an easy fix, of course. Some Ricearoni requires frying the noodles first before boiling, but has its own spices.

Realemon keeps well and makes a great drink even without ice as does Kool-Aid if you carry sugar. Realemon also great on fish.

Salt and pepper–don't forget them.

Appendix 3

The Improbable Jim Kurz Beats the Buffalo Ridge

By Brand Frentz

First published in *Minnesota Paddler*, a publication of the Minnesota Canoeing Association

A Strange Phone Call

In May 2005 I got a call from some guy I had never heard of named Jim. He said he was paddling up the Minnesota River past my house near Mankato.

"Where're you going?" I asked.

"Montana, Three Forks," he answered a little casually. I wondered if he was kidding.

I paused a minute and thought about it, then suggested: "I think you made a wrong turn."

"No, I'm gonna cross the Buffalo Ridge to the Missouri, go that way," he said matter-of-factly.

"I never heard of that way."

"Probably not, I just figured it out myself," said Jim Kurz.

The Buffalo Ridge

As the prairie sweeps west from the forests of Eastern Minnesota it meets a long, arcing rise in the land that the French explorers called the Coteau (Highlands) des Prairies. The crest of this ridge runs roughly parallel to and west of the Minnesota River, nearly 1,000 feet higher at some points. This landscape feature is now known as the Buffalo Ridge. It is heavily farmed – corn and beans. Local paddlers know some good whitewater stretches on the small rivers coming down the ridge, but no one I know has ever thought of crossing the ridge by canoe. Until Jim Kurz came along.

Clueless on a Lark

On April 13, 2005 Jim Kurz, a tall, raw-boned 60-year-old ex-professor and house painter, launched his ancient, overloaded 17-foot Grumman canoe with his dog Daisy perched in the bow on the Flambeau River outside his house in Ladysmith, Wisconsin. They were headed for Montana. "It was," he said, "that time in my life when I had to do something a little different. If I didn't do it then, I never would."

There was an odd name painted on the bow of his boat: "Clueless on a Lark." Jim did appear ill-prepared and he was definitely heading for an adventure with the unknown. But really the name concealed his own sly modesty. It was a play on the names of the explorers Lewis and Clark, who also went up the Missouri to Montana.

The Flambeau flows into the Chippewa, which flows into the Mississippi, and Jim knew he could go down to St. Louis and then up the Missouri. But he decided on "something different": turning right at the Mississippi and going up the Minnesota and tributaries and over the Buffalo Ridge to the Missouri drainage in South Dakota.

Jim studied the maps, talked with a few local people on the Ridge, and had a chance to drive through the area and look at some of the streams in February 2005. He decided that it could be done. By canoe. Take the Redwood River past Camden State Park to Coon Creek, follow that stream as far as possible, and then make a "fairly short" portage along roads to Lake Benton. Just beyond Lake Benton, cross the actual divide into the Flandreau Creek drainage, put in and paddle down to the Big Sioux and then the Missouri. He smiled when detractors called him "clueless."

Jim started up the Minnesota on April 28, struggling against high spring flows. As he made his way upstream it rained steadily and the river rose further. It was hard going, especially carrying a load of roughly 500 pounds counting man and dog. He passed river mile 150 at New Ulm on May 10, and in another week, against still-rising waters, he reached the point where the Redwood River feeds in.

This was the turning point for the Ridge. On May 17 Jim left the Minnesota and headed up the Redwood. For half a mile the river was broad and flat, then the rapids started, one after another, too swift to paddle or pole through, and no walkable bank for lining. He had to get out and wade, pulling the boat along by hand, through 15 rapids. Luckily the river was no more than waist deep. The four miles to the town of Redwood Falls took eight hours, and he was beat when he got to Ramsay Park. It was a rough start. Jim told himself, "Four miles down, 120 to go."

He took a layover in Redwood Falls, visited, rested, and did his first portage. Here we have to explain his load and his method of moving it. He was carrying everything but the kitchen sink, at least 250 pounds of gear (including a sailing frame and sail) and food piled up to the gunwales. Several five-gallon plastic tubs of dehydrated soup barely fit. But Jim didn't carry this load on his back; he pulled it on portage wheels. It was usually done in two rounds: one with his big cooler mounted on the axle frame and other items tucked around it, and the other with the canoe and all the remaining load in it. The wheels worked well on paved roads, and were usable on unpaved roads and smooth ground.

Redwood Falls has some steep hills, and Jim's route led right up one of them from the campground to the dam above the park. He moved the first two loads on the 18th and was lucky to meet Lever Deprez, a retired Belgian farmer who let Jim store his things in his yard. The canoe load was the heaviest, but Jim couldn't set it down because it wouldn't stand on the steep slope. He was bushed when he made the top.

The rest of the day was spent visiting in town. River keeper Jim Doering took him home and gave him a few of the things canoe trippers like best: a shower, laundry, and home-cooked food. He also stopped by the Madsen Vet Clinic (his vet knew Madsen). Daisy wanted to pick up some dog food, but when Jim saw the price he had to decline. The vet assistants quickly rushed around and gathered up three weeks of free samples for Daisy. In the evening he got a ride back to the campground and spent a second night there.

Over the Ridge – Two Grueling Weeks

In the morning of May 19 Jim portaged his camping gear to Lever's house, wheeled it all to the dam, and put his canoe in on the reservoir. A few miles of flat water were followed by some modest rapids that he lined. Progress was reasonable and soon the river leveled out. For the next few days the river was full and gentle, passing through farmland with no problems worse than an occasional low-head or beaver dam. Jim made new friends along the river and enjoyed taking it easy for a while and still making 10 miles a day.

By May 25 he reached Marshall, where shallow water had him poling. After passing a couple of dams in the channelized river running through town he came upon a friendly woman (a "shapely blonde with Irish brown eyes") working in her garden right next to the water. After a brief, friendly exchange Jim offered her a ride in his "gondola." She smiled, but decided not to climb into the middle of all that dehydrated soup. He poled on and camped on the west edge of town.

Things got rough after Marshall. The first day the river was narrower and Jim had to use his handy folding saw several times to saw through small (4") fallen tree trunks that blocked the channel. Toward evening, just short of Lynd, the rapids started again. The gradient increased the next day, making a stronger current, more rapids and more work. Jim barely made it to the lower campground in Camden State Park by evening. In the first two days out of Marshall he had covered about 10 miles.

But it didn't get easier. The next day, May 28, may have been the toughest of the crossing. Jim could see that it would be back-breaking and probably impossible to take the boat upstream fully loaded, so he put as much gear as he could with the cooler and wheeled the load up the park trail to the end. The trail had bumps and dips and steep climbs, about the limit for the portage wheels, but a family who walked with him helped out and made the time pass a little faster.

Coming back Jim started upstream in the partly unloaded (but still heavy) canoe. It was grueling work. He had to unload everything 10 times, man-haul the gear past the rapids, and then line the canoe through. There was a little poling and paddling mixed in now and then. When the long, exhausting day was over Jim was just past the park boundary. He had come two miles.

The next day was not much better. He only had to unload nine times, but it was the full boat. He struggled to get another two miles and made camp at the ball field in Russell. Jim says now that it was a mistake to come up the river past Lynd: he should have picked out the best roads and made the long portage from that town.

On Monday, May 30 Jim was ready to check out Coon Creek, which joins the Redwood River near Russell. The clerk at the local C-store told him that trying to paddle it would be insane and drove him along the creek to prove it. Jim had to agree, Coon Creek wasn't navigable. He would have to portage all the way to Lake Benton.

Fortunately, there is a county road that runs straight from Russell to the north shore of the lake. Unfortunately, it is a 14-mile trip.

Jim took it with the canoe load (it weighed a good 200 pounds, counting the boat), and then hiked back with the wheels. During this day-long trip several motorists offered him a ride, which he declined. One, Mark Wilmes of the Lake Benton News, stopped and interviewed him.

He slept at the ball field in Russell again that night, then loaded up the rest of his gear and trudged back to the lake. Once there, having done 42 miles of hauling in two days, he took the rest of the day off at the Tyler City Campground on the lake shore.

Jim reached the town of Lake Benton by sailing across the lake. He had now used every possible method of moving the canoe – from lining and wheeling to poling and paddling and now sailing – with the one exception of putting it on his shoulders and carrying in traditional voyageur style. Without the wheels he would have needed at least 6-8 rounds to get everything from point A to point B, i.e. 40-60 miles on the hoof.

There was a surprise when Jim picked up the newspaper in Lake Benton. He was on the front page; the story about him was already in print! It was a friendly town. On top of the press coverage, he was able to talk the town cop into letting him camp in the park, right by the "No Camping" sign. A good way to get ready for the actual crossing.

June 2 was the day that Jim went over the divide into the Missouri River drainage. There was no dramatic hill, just a gradual rise along US Highway 75. He wheeled the loaded canoe south, over the top, and then began coming to bridges over small, unpromising tributaries of Flandreau Creek, his chosen route. After about seven miles and still finding no suitable water, Jim headed west onto county roads. Finally on Pipestone County Road 11 he found a bridge from which the creek appeared navigable. It took the rest of the day to return to town and get the cooler load and bring it to the put-in. The total distance covered on foot this day was about 25 miles. Jim set up camp and took his well-earned rest right there.

June 3 and 4 were anticlimactic. Flandreau Creek was a small, winding stream but just big enough, just deep enough. As it grew he was able to paddle more or less normally. There were a couple of trees to cut away, but by the evening of June 4 Jim was camped at the confluence with the Big Sioux River. The Buffalo Ridge had been conquered and Jim Kurz had a few days of downstream travel before starting the long haul up the Missouri to Montana. Things were going just like he planned back in Ladysmith.

All's Well That Ends Well

On October 3, 2005 the old Grumman canoe carrying Jim and his faithful Lab Daisy reached Three Forks, Montana, the source of the Missouri River, marking the end of an amazing 1,744-mile upstream struggle. For frosting on the cake, after a couple of weeks of vacation he put back in on the Yellowstone and headed home, reaching North Dakota before winter stopped him.

Jim says today that he believes his route over the Buffalo Ridge was a good one and wonders if others will follow it now that he has blazed the trail. Not many will, I suspect.

Appendix 4

Photo Credits

All photos are mine except #070 by Malcolm Maxwell, #171 from Tom Garvey, #607 by James Clinton, #837 and #838 by Mike Su; #519 and #055 were copied off of the Internet at web sites I can't find anymore.

About the Author

#925 Author on the Yellowstone River

The author admits to having had a wonderful life so far, capped off by a 7 month canoe trip at the age of 60 in 2005. Born in 1945 in central Wisconsin, he and 5 siblings were introduced to America by their parents as they towed their home-made trailer home to California and even to Alaska on the gravel of the Alcan Highway in 1954. Other highlights include 30 years of happy marriage beginning in Madison, teaching chemistry in the Peace Corps in Colombia, a Ph. D. from Vanderbilt, 2 wonderful children born in Nashville and Denver, a short career in medical research in Denver and Chapel Hill, an even shorter stint of teaching college in Northwestern Wisconsin, and 20 years of knocking around Wisconsin as a self-employed handyman and painter. After his divorce in 1998 and the death of his last parent in 2004, he managed to break even with his debts and pay the rent for 8 months ahead, leaving him free to attempt every fisherman's dream, a long camping trip on the water. That story is told here.